CHAMPIONSHIP
paper
planes

D1337622

Paul Jackson

A MARY FORD BOOK

First published in Great Britain in 1998 by
MARY FORD BOOKS a division of
Michael O'Mara Books Limited, 9 Lion Yard,
Tremadoc Road, London SW4 7NQ

Cover design by Chris Leishman Design
Designed by Robert Updegraff
Photography by Meg Sullivan Photography
Typeset by Florencetype Limited
Printed and bound in Singapore by Tien Wah Press

ISBN 1-85479-356-X

Contents

Why Planes Fly

Principles of Flight	6
Stability	7

Basics

Papers to Use	9
The Best Way to Fold Paper Planes	9
Best Ways to Launch	11
"My Plane Won't Fly!"	12
Symbols	16
How to Make a Square	17
How to Make a 1:√2 Rectangle	18
Folding Techniques	19

Simple Designs

Wide Wing	24
Dove	26
Stacked over Logan	28
Fly Paper	30
The Scooter	32
Hanging Hawk	34
Pro Glider	36
Higby	38
Lock-nosed Plane	40
Bill Glider	42

ADVANCED DESIGNS

Immamura Special	44
Lock Dart	46
Chuck Finn	48
Stunt Plane	50
Needle Floater	52
The Cutter	54
Stealth Wing	56
Glynn's Glider	58
Thunder Bomber	60
Classique	62
Launch Assist	64

UNUSUAL DESIGNS

Swan	68
Butterfly	70
Sachet Glider	72
Sachet Stunt Plane	74
Bat	76
Human Cannonball	78
Gliding Swan	81
Helicopter	84
Twirly	86
Sycamore Seed	88

HOW TO DESIGN YOUR OWN PLANES 90

Acknowledgements	*96*
Origami Societies	*96*

Introduction

To rise above the earth and fly as free as a bird is a fantasy inside us all. Since earliest times in myth and in fact, people have tried to fly by mimicking the beating wings of a bird, but always without success. The efforts of the German glider designer, Otto Lillenthal (1848–96), established the wing shape necessary to create lift on a heavier-than-air *fixed wing* craft. Later, the American Wright brothers developed a motor-driven propeller powerful enough to keep a Lillenthal-type glider aloft, achieving the first powered flight in 1903 at Kittyhawk Sands, North Carolina, USA. Their achievement was a major turning point in human history.

And yet, for all the extraordinary advances in powered flight since then, the romance of unpowered flight remains. The grace of a pencil-thin glider riding the thermals or of a hang glider descending into a valley is a sight not quickly forgotten. For the more faint-hearted, the earthly equivalent of soaring silently through the air is to make and launch unpiloted gliders, and to watch them from the safety of terra firma.

Many people make model gliders from balsa wood and tissue; many others make gliders from paper and cardboard parts cut from books and glued together for strength. However, in truth, nothing can quite match the pleasure of taking an ordinary sheet of paper, making a few deft folds, then without the aid of glue, tape or weights, launching it with minimal effort and watching it glide smoothly through the air to a gentle landing.

The appeal of paper planes cuts across all ages and cultures, I think for several reasons. Firstly, the speed and simplicity of the means – just simple folds in ordinary paper, nothing else. Secondly, the reassuringly clear way in which success or failure can be assessed – either a plane flies well or it doesn't, there are no troublesome conundrums about "meaning" or "beauty". Thirdly, paper planes appeal to different people for different reasons – as art, science, magic, social prop, school game, creative challenge, etc. And fourthly, because the graceful sight of a paper plane in flight is a temporary release from our earthly responsibilities – a moment of innocent delight and mystery. Add these reasons together and the popularity of paper planes is easy to understand.

This book presents a collection of designs from around the world, intended to appeal both to the beginner and to the experienced enthusiast, eager to make new designs. If you are new to making paper planes, please read the *Basics* chapter with care. It will give you many useful tips on folding and flying, plus a little about the basics of origami. In addition, beginners should be wary of trying to fold the more complex designs too early – this often ends in frustration and can be dispiriting. But that said, taking on a major challenge can sometimes be fun!

When folding a design – simple or complex – it is most important to understand that however frivolous folding paper planes may seem, a good flier is the result of good science. Only those planes folded and flown with attention to detail will fly well. So, although the primary purpose of this book is to entertain, please remember that the more care you put into the folding, the more fun you'll have from the flying.

I've had many hours of great enjoyment designing, researching and testing the paper planes in this book. It is my sincere wish that you will have just as much pleasure from making and flying them.

Happy landings!

Paul Jackson

Why planes fly

Just why a *real* plane flies is a wonder of the modern age and of course, a paper plane flies following the same principles.

This chapter describes in general terms the two *Principles of Flight*, which explain why a plane stays in the air, followed by a description of how to eliminate pitching, rolling and yawing to achieve *Stability* in flight. The casual reader may wish to skip these pages, but a basic knowledge of why a plane flies and how it can be made to fly well will greatly increase your enjoyment of making and flying paper planes, and will help correct poor flying performances.

Principles of Flight

One "*The forward thrust must be greater than the drag.*"

In other words, an aerodynamic shape will enable a plane to cut efficiently through the air.

The effect of drag can be demonstrated easily with a sheet of paper. Hold it as shown so that it hangs vertically, then move your hand to the left. The entire front surface of the paper is presented to the air as the hand moves, so drag is maximised. Indeed, the bottom edge bends upwards in an attempt to reduce drag.

Repeat, but now flick your wrist so that the paper is pulled horizontally through the air like a magic carpet. Notice how drag is minimised.

So, put simply, a plane will fly better if it is designed to cut through the air, rather than resist it. In other words, a paper plane should present thin edges to the air that it flies through, not flat surfaces. When seen from the front, a plane should be as invisible as possible.

However, although a minimal profile will reduce drag, a plane will not fly if the thrust is small. Thrust is provided by throwing or dropping the plane. When thrust is greater than drag, a plane will fly, though the friction of the air moving over the plane will eventually slow it to a standstill and gravity will bring it to earth.

Two *"The lift from the wings must be greater than the effect of gravity."*

Just why a wing causes a plane to lift is difficult to comprehend – indeed, this lack of understanding gives many potential air passengers a disabling fear of flying.

Put simply, if the pressure of air below the wing is greater than the pressure above it, the wing will lift. Air pressure is reduced by increasing the speed of airflow, so that if the air travels faster above the wing than below it, lift is generated. This is achieved simply by arching the top surface of the wing and flattening the bottom surface, so that the air has to travel a greater distance at a greater speed over the top surface than under the bottom one. In this way, lift is created.

This abstract theorem can be demonstrated by blowing down onto a strip of paper. Surprisingly, the strip *lifts*! This is because the blowing has made the air move faster across the top surface than across the bottom surface, reducing air pressure and causing the paper to lift. Try it.

Stability

A plane which adheres to the **Principles of Flight** described above may still be unstable. An unstable plane may roll, pitch or yaw, and there are different ways to remedy each, shown here. To demonstrate the instabilities and to show the corrections, a stylised flat plane design is used as an example.

Roll

A plane rolls when it rotates around its lateral axis, so that as one wing dips the other rises, causing the plane to corkscrew. The way to correct this is to make a crease down the centre to create a small angle between the wings, called the "dihedral" angle. With the addition of this crease, the plane will rock to and fro, but will not corkscrew as before.

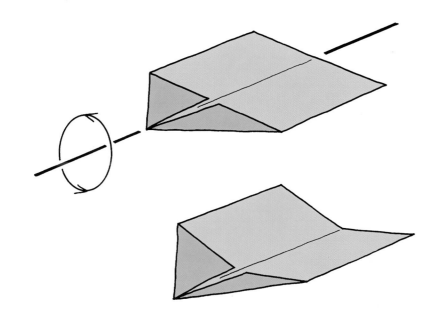

Pitch

A plane pitches when it rotates around its longitudinal axis, so that the nose rises or dips. The way to correct this is to bend the trailing corners of the wings upwards for a downward dip (a nose-dive) or downward for an upwards rise (stalling).

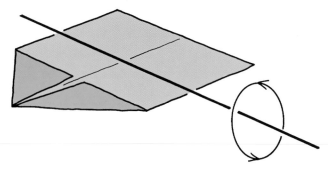

To correct a dipping nose

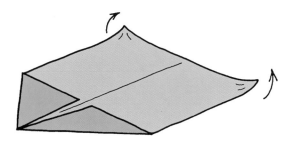

To correct a rising nose

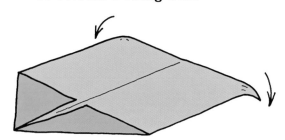

Yaw

A plane yaws when it rotates around its latitudinal axis, so that it flies in circles. The way to correct this is to create a vertical surface to provide resistance against the yawing. This is usually done by creating a fuselage or rudders at the wing tips, or sometimes both.

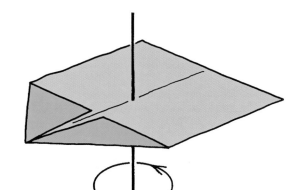

Fuselage

Rudders

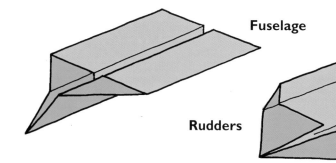

To prevent a roll, pitch or yaw, it is usual to incorporate all three corrections into the same design. A design with just one correction will not be as stable as a design with two or with all three, though some designs perform well with just one or two.

So, our unstable, flat plane could be completed with a dihedral angle to prevent rolling, bent trailing wing edges to prevent pitching (nose-diving or stalling) and a fuselage or rudders to prevent yawing.

Corrected plane

With the correct angle of launch and correct speed of throw – and a little subsequent trimming – it should fly well. And remember, if despite everything, your plane remains stubbornly unstable, you can always describe it as a "Stunt Special"!

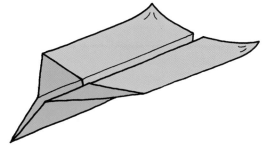

Basics

Papers to Use

There is no single "best" paper for paper planes. There are, however, several types of paper which should definitely *not* be used. In particular, papers which do not hold a crease well should be avoided, including newspaper, facial tissues and paper towels. These papers relax after being creased, ruining an aerodynamic profile.

Heavy papers of any type should also be avoided. They are simply too heavy to sustain prolonged flight, though you may wish to experiment with such papers if you want to make giant planes, because lighter weights tend to collapse at an extreme scale. So, avoid heavier weights such as drawing paper, pastel paper and watercolour paper.

In general though, any paper about the weight of a page in this book, or a little lighter, may be used. This includes most of the inexpensive easily available papers such as photocopy paper, typing paper, writing paper and computer paper. If you intend to make many paper planes, it is good value to buy thick packets of your chosen paper from a stationer or small printer. My own preference is photocopy paper: it folds excellently, is very inexpensive, is ideally proportioned and comes in a range of attractive colours for extra appeal. Most small printers and walk-in photocopy shops sell a wide range of photocopy papers and also have an electric guillotine which can cut a block of rectangular sheets to perfect squares at nominal cost, saving you much labour and eliminating the possibility of making those frustratingly nearly square squares!

Try using unusual papers too. This almost endless list could include patterned gift-wrap paper, junk mail, paper-backed metallic foil, quality colour magazine paper, thin tracing paper, lightweight handmade paper and even disposable tablecloths. The rule here is simple: if in doubt, try it! You may be surprised at how well a plane flies when made from an unlikely paper — indeed, such papers give any plane a "presence" that ordinary photocopy papers can never give.

Always store paper horizontally and flat, preferably away from humid or damp air. Discard sheets which have dog-eared corners or crescent-shaped buckle marks, unless you know the damaged areas will be buried deep inside the layers of the nose, where they cannot disturb the smooth flow of air over the surface of the paper.

The Best Way to Fold Paper Planes

This section may seem unnecessarily dictatorial, but I am convinced that folding paper planes demands more care than folding other types of origami models, and that some of these finesses need explanation. So, please read the following paragraphs with care, even if you are an experienced paper folder.

Fold on a hard surface

Make *all* creases against a hard, level surface, such as a table top or a large hardback book. Never fold entirely in the air, on your lap or on a soft surface such as a carpet.

Fold accurately and with care

Paper planes will only fly well if they are folded slowly, with great attention to detail and with great accuracy. So, at all stages, check that your folding is exactly symmetrical, that sharp points are absolutely sharp and that delicate single thickness wings are never accidentally bent out of shape.

Press firmly

All creases must be made firmly to help the edges cut cleanly through the air. It helps to fold smoothly and with confidence, so consider your first attempt at folding a new design to be a dress rehearsal, not a definitive performance.

Smooth flat the layers

In some designs, the building up of bulky layers towards the nose and/or along the leading edge of the wings means that the paper will not lie absolutely flat against the hard folding surface beneath, but begins to bubble upwards as though air was trapped inside. This bubbling increases the cross-section of the plane in flight and will adversely affect performance.

The remedy is to smooth down the layers after each step. Start at the centre crease and press the paper down firmly, stroking left and right towards the nose and leading edges of the wings. The crease along the leading edge will move very slightly as the paper is flattened, but this is normal.

Here is an example:

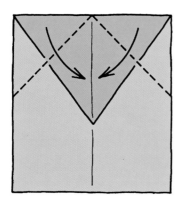
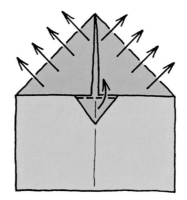

**Stroke the paper outwards
to flatten it.**

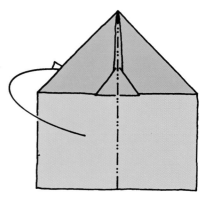

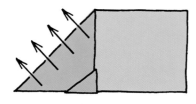

**Stroke the paper
outwards to flatten it.**

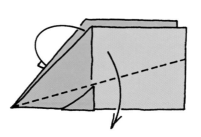
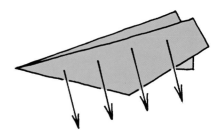

**Stroke the paper
outwards to flatten it.**

Best Ways to Launch

There is much more to successfully launching a paper plane than holding it in any position, with any grip and releasing it with any throwing action. Just as there are different grips and swings in golf, each paper plane must be held and thrown in the correct way to achieve the best result. Indeed, one experienced paper plane friend of mine believes that if he only knew how to throw it, he could make a house brick glide gracefully into the distance! He was joking of course, but the point was well made.

Here then are a few general tips on holding and throwing.

Holding

Experiment throwing a plane by holding it in different places along the fuselage.

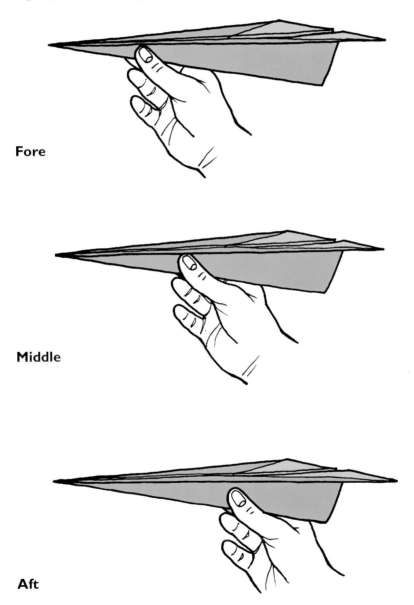

Fore

Middle

Aft

Generally, the best position is around the centre of balance – the point where the plane will balance in your hand without tipping – though it is important to try other positions for comparison.

Speed

The tendency amongst the inexperienced is to throw a paper plane either too gently, so that it never catches the air and wafts sleepily to the ground, or with so much force that it careers swiftly through the air for a short distance, without forming an aerodynamic profile, before crashing violently. Most planes need launching with moderate force, though it is always worth experimenting with other speeds and with what your perception of "moderate" means.

Launch angle

The four main angles of launch are vertically upward, diagonally upward, horizontal and downward.

Vertically upward is an unpredictable launch, best executed with speed and athleticism. The intention is to hurl the plane as high as possible before it starts to level out and begins its (hopefully) slow descent. Clearly, a room with a very high ceiling is necessary for this launch, or perhaps a calm day outdoors, but success is limited. Performed well though, this is the technique that sets world records for duration and distance and is worth trying just for the fun of it.

Diagonally upward at an angle between 30° and 45° to the horizontal is the most common and versatile launch angle. When thrown at moderate speeds, most planes will perform well. Experiment with the precise angle of launch, as too steep an angle may make a plane stall and too shallow an angle may reduce the duration or distance of the flight.

Horizontal launching creates steady, unspectacular flights and is best for delicate gliders in confined spaces. Almost all planes will fly when launched in this way, but will probably fly better if launched at a different angle.

Downward launching may seem perverse, but can create excellent acrobatic flights. Try it! If the plane nose-dives heavily to the ground, simply curl up the trailing edges of the wings. This creates the extra lift that will bend its flight path upwards. It is important to throw always with considerable speed, never gently.

"My Plane Won't Fly!"

How often I have heard this remark! The truth is that planes *rarely* fly well on a first throw. That first throw is a test to see how it performs: does it nose-dive, stall, or what? Once the problem is noted, a solution can be attempted. However, it is important to remember that planes are unfailingly temperamental. A plane that dives when one person throws it may stall when someone else throws it, or a plane that glides majestically into the distance on a first throw may never do so again. So, if improving the flight characteristics of a plane sometimes proves enigmatic, don't be disheartened – we all have the same problem.

There are, however, several reliable ways to improve a performance. By experimenting, learning from experience and having a little luck, the ideal combination of trimming and launching can make even the most desperate no-hoper fly reasonably, even superbly.

So, before consigning a plane to oblivion, try these remedies.

Dihedral

This is the angle that the wings make across the top of the fuselage. Generally, a plane flies best when its wings are horizontal in flight, which means that the dihedral forms a shallow V-shape when the fuselage is pinched shut immediately prior to launching.

Dihedral when held in the hand   **The same plane in flight**

It is a common error to have the wings level when the plane is held in the hand, so that they point downward when the plane is in flight, thus:

Dihedral when held in the hand   **The same plane in flight**

Slight adjustment of the dihedral can dramatically affect performance. For example:

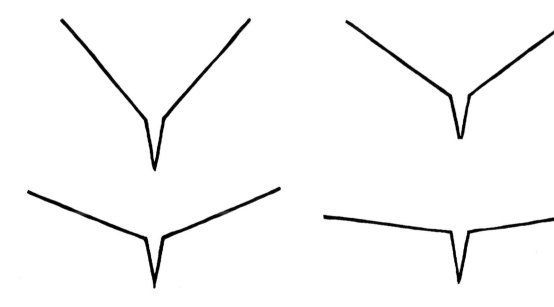

So, if your plane is not flying well, the first and simplest adjustment to make is to change the angle of dihedral.

Stalling

Stalling occurs when the plane flies upwards, stops (or "stalls") and drops like a stone. The usual cause is either because the nose is too light or the back half of the plane is too heavy. In other words, the plane's centre of gravity is too far back and should be moved forward.

The simplest and quickest remedy is to bend the trailing edges of the wings *downward*, thus:

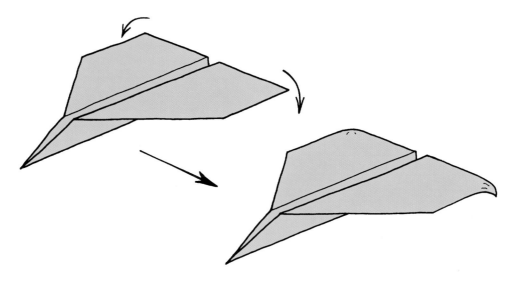

The more they are bent, the more the stalling will be compensated for, so the degree of bend is absolutely critical for a level flight. If the plane still stalls, bend more; if it nose-dives, unbend a little. Done well, this simple technique is extremely effective.

If no amount of bending will compensate for the stalling, try bulking up the layers at the nose by folding it back on itself once or twice, thus:

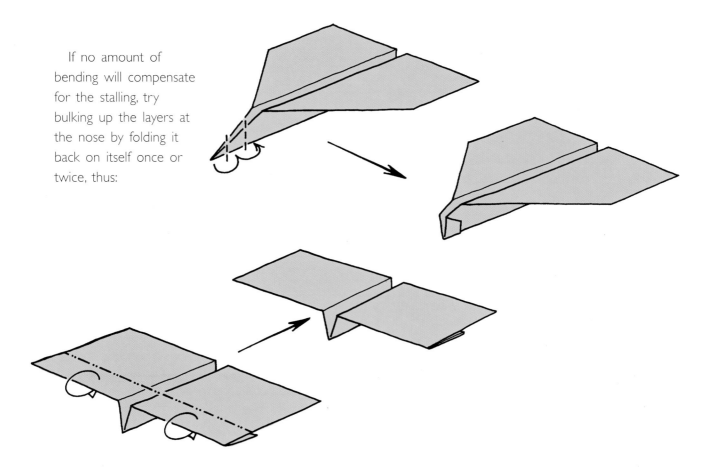

With some designs, this folding back remedy is not always possible, so instead, try adding Blu-Tack or paperclips to the nose, thus:

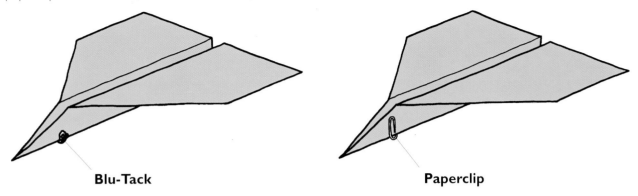

Blu-Tack   **Paperclip**

The position and exact weight of the paperclip(s) or Blu-Tack is critical, so experiment to achieve a level flight.

Nose-diving

Nose-diving occurs when the plane flies downward. The cause is the opposite to stalling: when it nose-dives, either the nose is too heavy or the back half is too light, so that the centre of gravity is too far forward.

The only truly effective remedy is to bend the trailing edges of the wings *upwards*, thus:

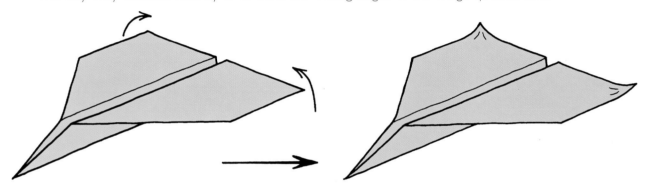

The more they are bent, the more the nose-diving will be compensated for, so the degree of bend is absolutely critical for a level flight. You will probably find that *most* planes need a small upward bend of the trailing edge, regardless of design, so be prepared to do this.

Other remedies

If the remedies suggested above fail to work, try these:

Holding. Experiment with holding the plane further forward or further back (see "Holding", p. 11).

Speed of launch. Experiment with faster and slower launch speeds (see "Speed", p. 12).

Angle of launch. Experiment with a higher or flatter angle of launch (see "Launch angle", p. 12).

Summary

Planes, remember, are temperamental. If your plane doesn't fly well on its maiden flight, one of the remedies suggested above should work just on its own, so work through them methodically. Sometimes the solution is a combination of remedies. You may need to increase or decrease the dihedral, *and* bend the trailing edges of the wings up or down, *and* throw your plane faster or slower than before. These experiments can all be done in seconds and with just a few test flights. That said, finding just the right combination of remedies can sometimes be frustrating, and a newly folded plane that flew well a minute ago might not be coaxed into a repeat performance and is best folded again from a fresh sheet.

With experience, you will come to learn that a performance can rarely be predicted, but just hoped for and worked towards. Along the way, a ripe sense of the ridiculous will be very helpful!

Symbols

The following symbols are used throughout the book to explain how the paper moves when folded.

It is important to keep looking ahead to the next step to see the results of the present step. Thus, the steps are a series of interlocking links, each one being the product of the previous step's instructions and giving instructions to proceed to the next. So, never look at each step in isolation, but *keep looking ahead*. Also, be sure to follow *every* symbol on *every* step, so fold slowly and with attention to detail.

The symbols need not all be learnt now, but it is important, at least, to know the difference between a valley fold and a mountain fold before folding. When you come across an unfamiliar symbol, refer back to this table.

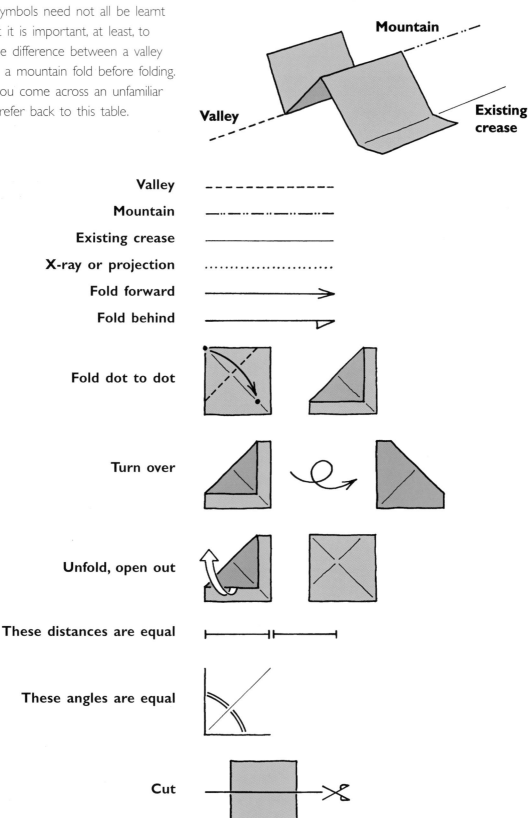

Valley	– – – – – – – – –
Mountain	—··—··—··—··—··—
Existing crease	————————
X-ray or projection	··························
Fold forward	————————➤
Fold behind	————————▷
Fold dot to dot	
Turn over	
Unfold, open out	
These distances are equal	
These angles are equal	
Cut	

How to Make a Square

Most bought papers are rectangular and need trimming for those planes that are folded from a square.

There are two methods for making a square:

I. A square with a diagonal crease

This method is suitable for those planes requiring a diagonal crease.

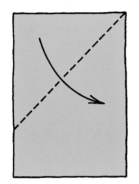 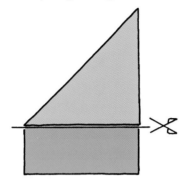 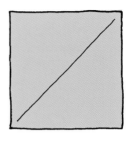

Fold over a triangle   **Cut off the rectangle**   **Here is the square with its diagonal crease**

2. A square without a diagonal crease

This method is suitable for those planes which do not require a diagonal crease.

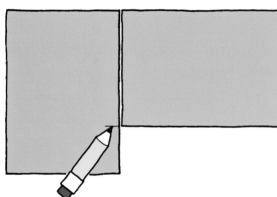 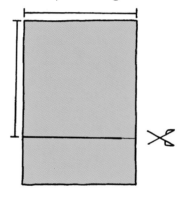 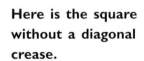

Carefully line up two sheets as shown, then draw a short line at the edge of the upright sheet.   **Make a crease across the paper at the level of the mark.**   **Cut off the rectangle.**   **Here is the square without a diagonal crease.**

If only one sheet is available, the method is a little different.

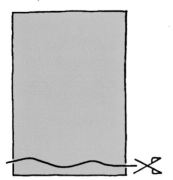 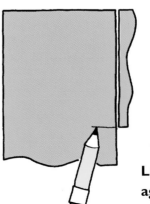 

Cut off a narrow edge along the bottom. The cut need not be straight.   **Lay the cut piece against the rectangle and continue as above.**

How to Make a 1:√2 Rectangle

The 1:√2 rectangle is the standard paper proportion used throughout the world, except in the USA where the 8½ x 11in (Letter size) and 11 x 17in (Legal size) still prevail. The 1:√2 rectangle is more commonly referred to by its "A" size: A1, A2, A3, A4, A5, etc., of which by far the most common is "A4", (210 x 297mm) used in photocopiers, and a close equivalent to 8½ x 11in paper.

Its shape can be explained by saying that if a square has a side length of 1, then by Pythagoras, the diagonal will be √2 (or 1.414 ...). The diagonal can be swung to the vertical to locate point C:
An "A" proportioned rectangle can then be constructed from point C, so that if its short side is 1, its long side is √2.
The important advantage of this shape over any other (including 8½ x 11in paper) is that when it is folded or cut across the middle, each half **remains a 1:√2 rectangle.** ... etc.

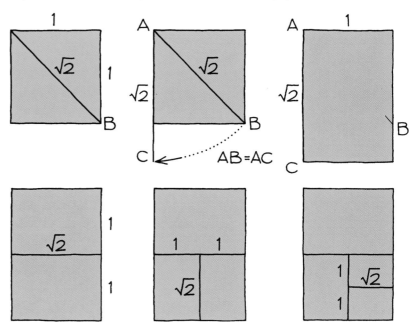

No other rectangular proportion is self-repeating when halved or doubled. This makes it the perfect rectangle to fold because creases and proportions have a beautiful habit of coinciding or being equal, making a folding sequence both logical and elegant.

A4 is very easy to find unless you live in the USA. So, for hapless US readers stuck somewhere in the Middle Ages with their 8½ x 11in paper, here is the best way to convert 8½ x 11in to a 1:√2 rectangle.

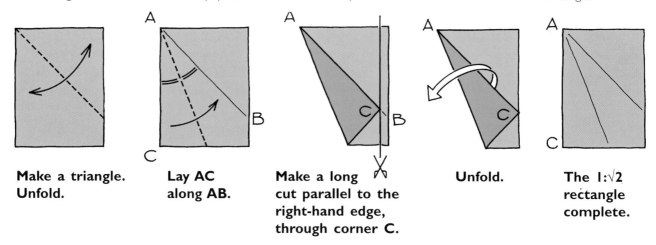

Make a triangle. Unfold.

Lay AC along AB.

Make a long cut parallel to the right-hand edge, through corner C.

Unfold.

The 1:√2 rectangle complete.

All the planes in the book will fly perfectly well when made from 8½ x 11in paper. However, the paper in the drawings is proportioned 1:√2, so readers folding 8½ x 11in paper will occasionally find their planes looking a little different to the drawings and may have to adjust a few of the folds to maintain alignments.

The solution for 8½ x 11in users is always to convert your paper to a 1:√2 rectangle by the method given above.

Folding Techniques

The basic single crease known as the "valley fold" and its opposite, the "mountain fold" require no explanation: they are not techniques but the fundamental element of folding. Techniques are established when two or more creases are manipulated simultaneously so that the process of folding becomes more complex.

These techniques can be grouped and named. In this book, techniques commonly known as the Squash Fold, Inside Reverse Fold and Outside Reverse Fold are used. Rather than explain them slowly each time they occur, it is more concise to explain them together and just once, here in the Basics section of the book.

So, if you are unfamiliar with Squash and Reverse folds, please practise these exercises.

Squash Fold

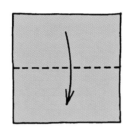

Fold in half.

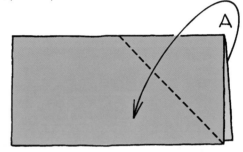

Make a diagonal crease, lifting corner A.

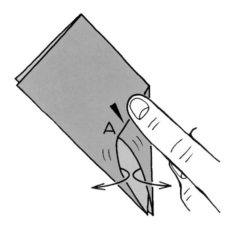

Put pressure on the edge behind A, opening the pocket.

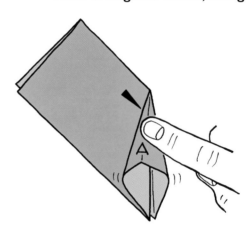

Squash A flat and crease firmly.

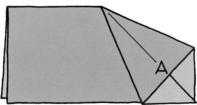

The Squash fold complete.

In the book, a Squash fold is diagrammed like this:

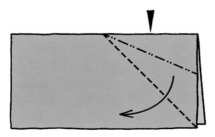

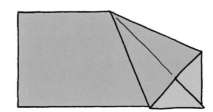

Inside Reverse Fold

Version A

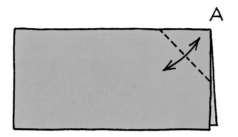

Begin with Step 2 of the Squash fold, then crease and unfold as shown.

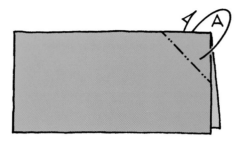

Mountain fold and unfold along the existing valley fold line.

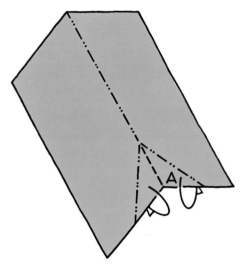

Separately crease three mountains and one valley as shown.

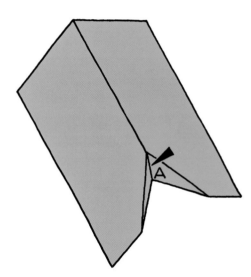

Fold the sheet in half again, but allowing corner **A** to collapse inside between the layers, out of sight.

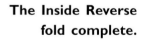

The Inside Reverse fold complete.

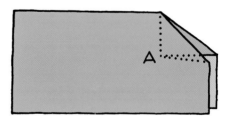

In this book, this version of the Inside Reverse fold is diagrammed thus:

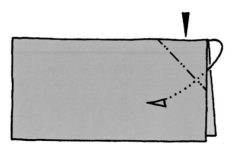
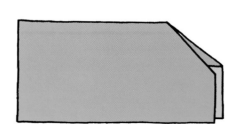

Version B

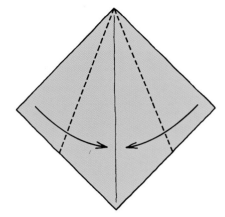

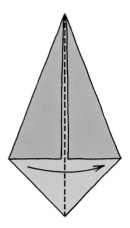

Fold the top edges to an existing centre crease.

Fold in half.

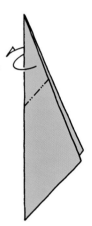

Valley and unfold.

Mountain and unfold along the existing valley fold line.

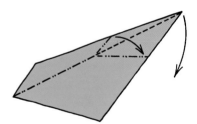

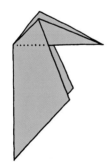

Separately crease three mountains and one valley as shown.

Fold in half, collapsing the creases.

The Inside Reverse fold complete.

In the book, this version of the Inside Reverse fold is diagrammed thus:

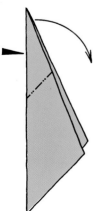

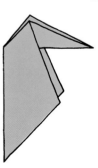

Outside Reverse Fold

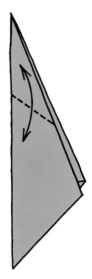 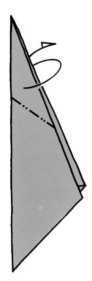 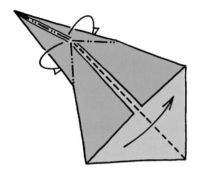

Begin with Step 3 of Version B of the Inside Reverse fold, then valley and unfold as shown.

Mountain fold and unfold along the existing valley fold line.

Form three mountains and one valley as shown, then fold the paper in half to collapse all the creases.

The Outside Reverse fold complete.

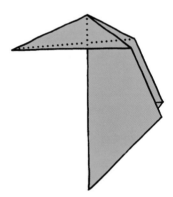

In this book, the Outside Reverse fold is diagrammed thus:

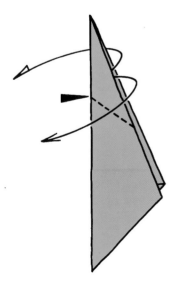 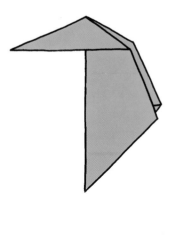

Simple Designs

The word "simple" is perhaps misleading, implying an uninteresting, basic design. In fact, a good, simple paper plane is a design of great refinement, distilling into a few folds the essence of an aerodynamic form. Also, the simple shapes of a simple design mean that such a plane will cut efficiently through the air, whereas a more complex design may create turbulence. Thus, simple designs are usually the best fliers.

Wide Wing

The extreme width of this design, relative to its length, means that it will glide slowly through the air like a soaring bird of prey. *Designed by Paul Jackson, UK.*

Use A4 or 8½ x 11 in paper.

1

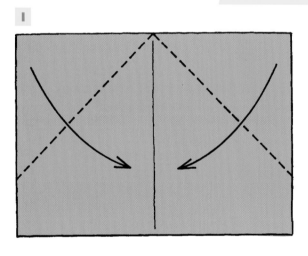

2

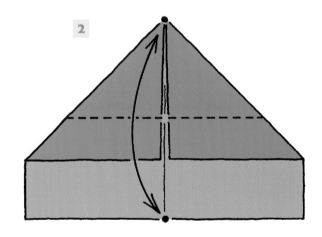

3

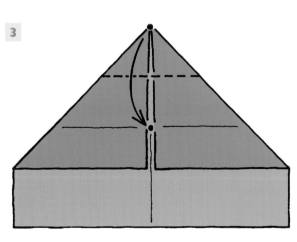

4

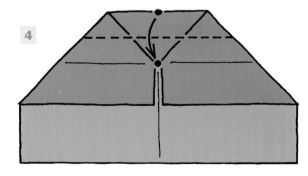

1. Crease and unfold the shorter centre crease, then bring the top corners to the crease.

2. Crease and unfold, dot to dot.

3. Fold dot to dot.

4. Again, fold dot to dot.

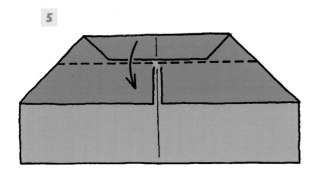

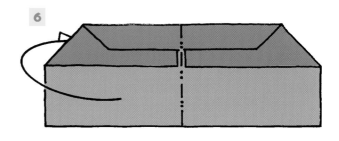

5. Fold over along the Step 2 crease.

6. Mountain fold the paper in half.

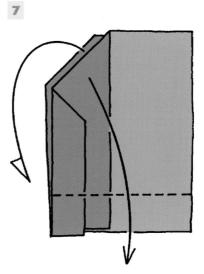

7. Create the wings, making sure that both creases are parallel to the bottom edge. The distance of the creases from the bottom edge is not critical.

8. The Wide Wing is complete.

Throwing Tip

Launch smoothly. If it fails to fly well, see "My Plane Won't Fly!" (p. 12) for advice.

Dove

This agreeably simple design flies superbly and with tremendous grace, though it is only barely dove-like in shape. With a little extra folding at the nose, recognisable head shapes can be created.   *Traditional Japanese.*

Use a 15–20cm (6–8in) square of thin paper.

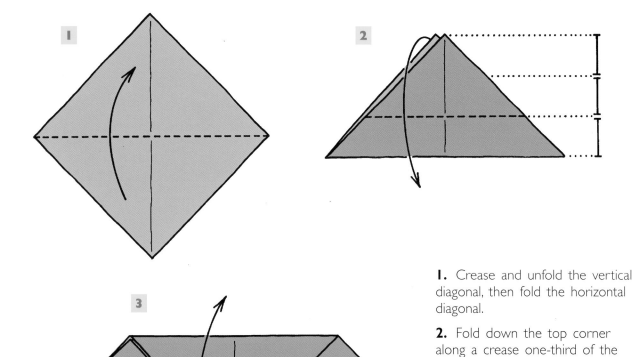

1. Crease and unfold the vertical diagonal, then fold the horizontal diagonal.

2. Fold down the top corner along a crease one-third of the distance between the bottom edge and the top corner.

3. Fold up the top layer only along a crease placed exactly where shown.

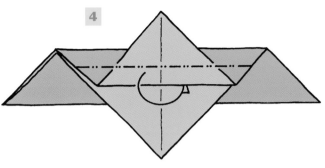

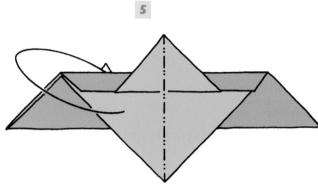

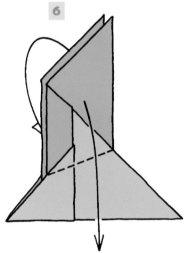

4. Mountain fold the loose edge out of sight, tucking it as far behind as it can go.

5. Mountain fold the paper in half.

6. Fold the nearside wing down along a crease that connects where the nose triangle passes over the leading edge of the wing, and the angle where the trailing edge of the wing passes behind the tail triangle. Repeat behind.

Throwing Tip

To launch, place your first finger on top of the central crease and release with a smooth flick.

7. The Dove is complete.

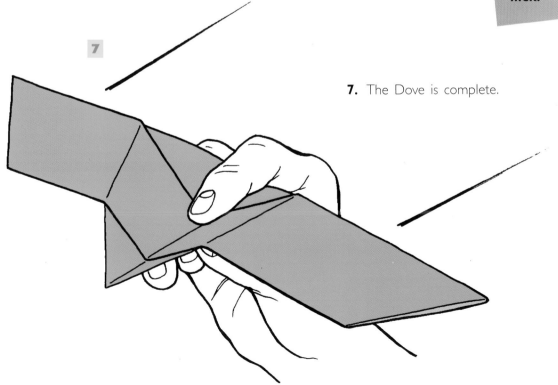

Stacked over Logan

Here is a design so simple in construction and appearance that it should not fly – but does! Its wafer-like shape means that several can be stacked and launched together to create a wonderful starburst effect. *Designed by Michael LaFosse, USA.*

Use a square of paper

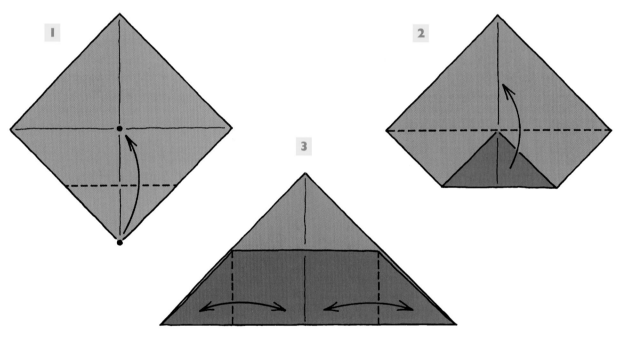

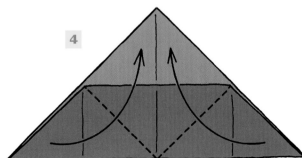

1. Crease and unfold both diagonals, then fold the bottom corner to the centre.

2. Fold over along the diagonal.

3. Fold in the corners to the centre line. Unfold.

4. Fold the bottom corners up to the top corner.

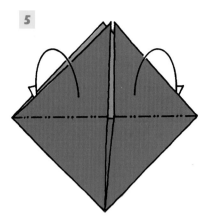

5. Using the Step 3 creases, tuck the loose corners into the pocket behind. This locks the paper flat.

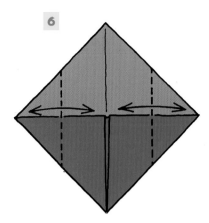

6. Fold the left and right corners to the centre point. Unfold.

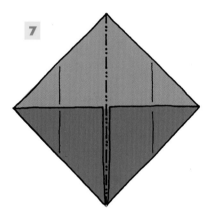

7. Mountain fold down the centre.

8. Adjust the creases to this profile.

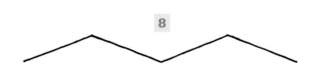

9. Stacked Over Logan is complete.

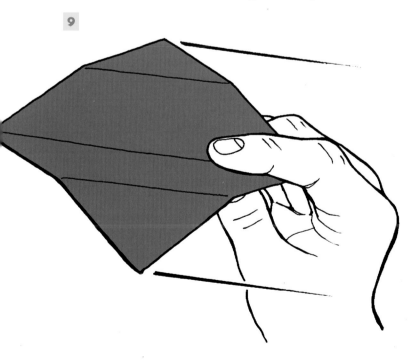

Throwing Tip

To launch, place your first finger on top of the centre crease and flick smoothly forwards.

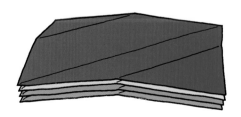

An entertaining variation is to make several and stack them neatly together. Launch by flicking them high into the air . . . and watch them scatter in all directions!

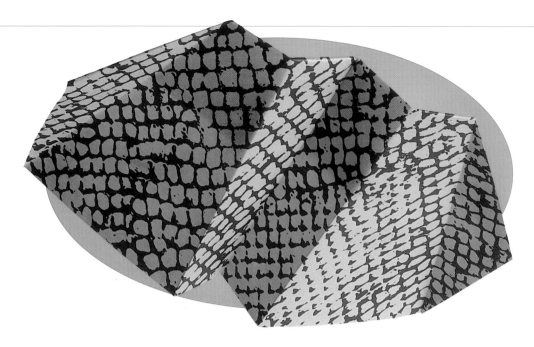

Fly Paper

Most paper planes are folded symmetrically, whereas this one is not. Despite the weight imbalance between the two sides of the finished design, it flies straight and true rather than round in circles, as might be supposed.   *Designed by Paul Jackson, UK.*

Use A4 or 8¹/₂ x 11in paper trimmed to a 1:√2 rectangle.

1

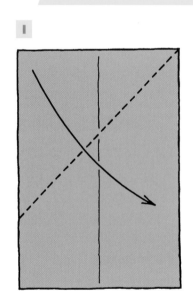

2

A

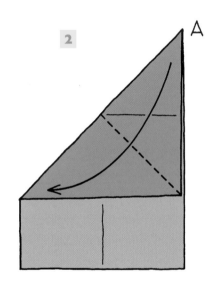

3

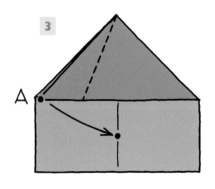

A

1. Crease and unfold the centre crease, then bring the top left-hand corner across to the right-hand edge and crease.

2. Fold corner A across to the left.

3. Fold corner A down to the centre crease.

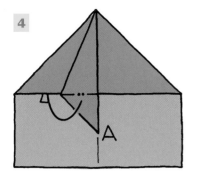

4. Tuck corner A out of sight.

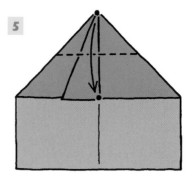

5. Fold dot to dot.

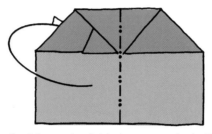

6. Mountain fold the paper in half.

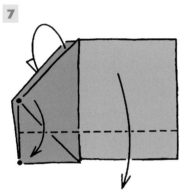

7. Fold dot to dot as shown, so that the crease is parallel to the bottom edge. Repeat behind.

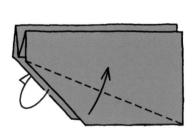

8. Fold up a triangle as shown. Repeat behind.

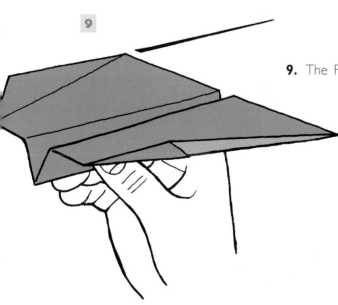

9. The Fly Paper is complete.

Throwing Tip

Hold and launch conventionally. If it fails to fly well, see "My Plane Won't Fly!" (p. 12) for advice.

The Scooter

Few designs feature a split wing, but the one created here enables the craft to cleave its way recklessly through the air. Take care to fold Step 2 with accuracy.　　*Designed by Paul Jackson, UK.*

Use A4 or 8¹/₂ x 11in paper

1

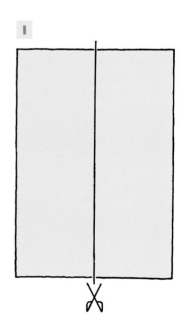

1. Cut the paper in half.

2. Fold dot to (imaginary) dot, so that triangle ABC is equilateral (all the sides are the same length).

3. Fold in half. Unfold.

4. Fold dot to dot. Unfold.

2

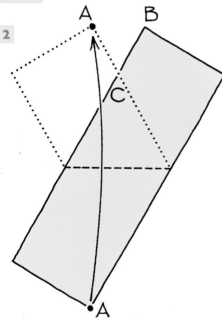

3

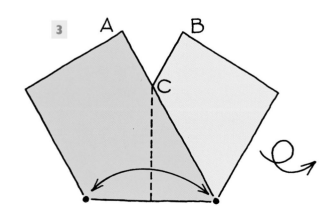

4

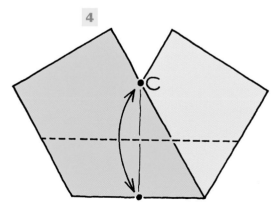

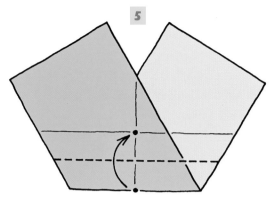

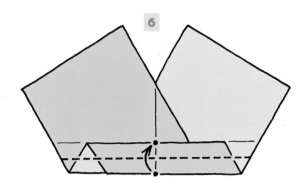

5. Again, fold dot to dot.

6. And again, dot to dot.

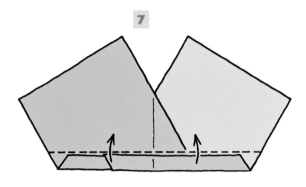

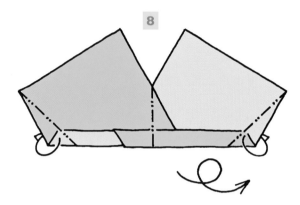

7. Fold over along the Step 4 crease.

8. Fold the bottom corner behind.

9. Adjust the central crease to this angle of dihedral.

10. The Scooter is complete.

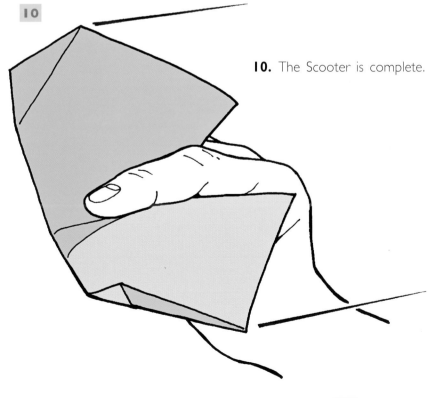

Throwing Tip

To launch, place your first finger on top of the centre crease and flick smoothly forwards.

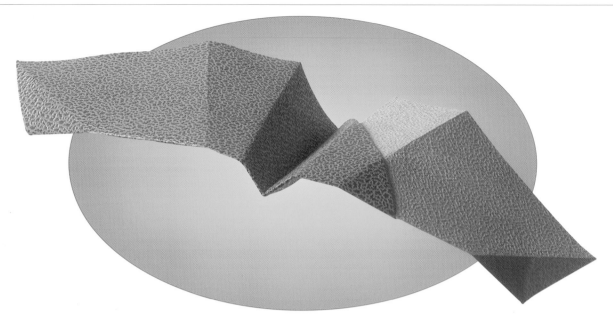

Hanging Hawk

The complex wing structure needs careful adjustment for this design to fly well, but your diligence will be well rewarded.   *Designed by Stephen Weiss, USA.*

Use A4 or 8¹/₂ x 11in paper trimmed to a 1:√2 rectangle.

1

2

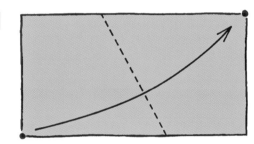

1. Trim off one-quarter of the width of the paper.

2. Turn the paper sideways, then fold the bottom left-hand corner up to the top right-hand corner.

3. Fold dot to dot as shown, ensuring that the crease is parallel to the bottom edge. Unfold.

4. Fold the bottom edge up to the existing crease.

3

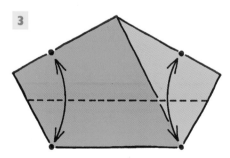

4

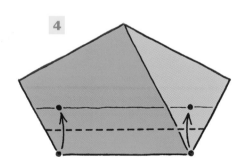

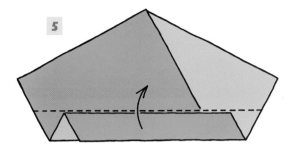

5. Roll over along the Step 3 crease.

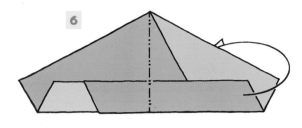

6. Mountain fold the paper in half.

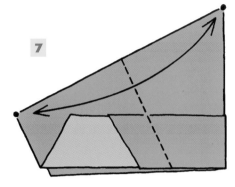

7. Fold dot to dot. Unfold. Repeat behind.

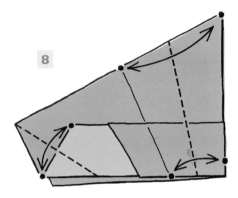

8. Fold the middle pair of dots over to lie on top of the right-hand pair. Unfold. Fold and unfold dot to dot at the left. Repeat everything behind.

9. Adjust the creases to create this profile.

10. The Hanging Hawk is complete.

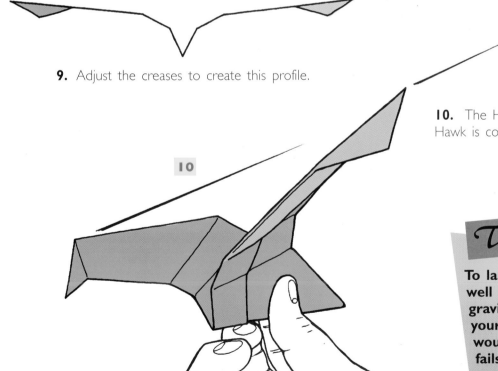

Throwing Tip

To launch, hold the design well behind the centre of gravity (if you loosened your grip, the Hawk would tip forwards). If it fails to fly well, experiment with the Step 9 profile.

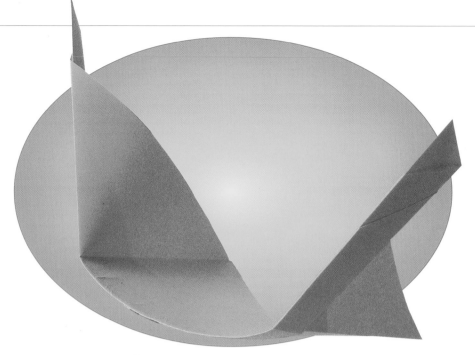

Pro Glider

This bizarre craft is actually an excellent flier! Launched accurately, it will glide a considerable distance, astonishing all those who assume that paper fliers must be "plane" shaped.
Designed by John Smith, UK.

Use A4 or 8½ x 11 in paper.

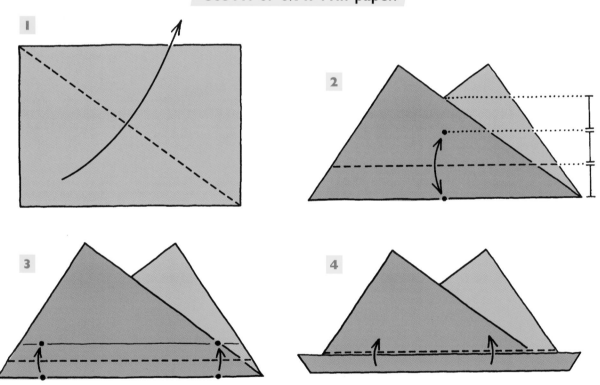

1. Crease the diagonal between the top left-hand and bottom right-hand corners. This can be awkward, so take your time.

2. Fold up the bottom edge to a point, one-third of the way between the notch and the bottom edge. Unfold.

3. Fold the bottom edge up to the Step 2 crease.

4. Fold over along the Step 2 crease.

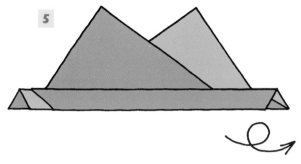

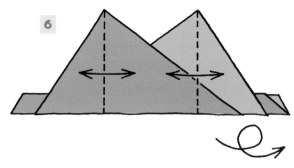

5. Turn over.

6. Make the vertical creases as shown. Turn over.

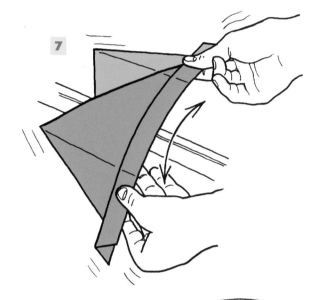

7. With the thick band on top, roll the section between the Step 6 creases over the edge of a table. This takes a little strength, so don't be too delicate!

8. Seen from the front, this is the result. Note the straight, vertical edges flanking the curved central section.

9. The Pro Glider is complete.

Throwing Tip

To launch, put your middle finger onto the top surface of the central section and your first and third fingers underneath to support it. Then, gently flick the Pro Glider horizontally forward. Try to do this as smoothly as possible, but not too slowly – extra speed will give a much longer flight.

Higby

The Squash fold in Step 9 creates a hollow pocket under the wing which – unusually – does not disrupt the aerodynamic profile, but assists it. A curious and creative technique!   *Designed by Stephen Weiss, USA*

Use A4 paper or 8½ x 11in paper trimmed to a 1:√2 rectangle.

1. Trim off one-sixth of the width of the paper.

2. Fold in half horizontally and vertically, unfolding each crease.

3. Fold the top edge to the centre.

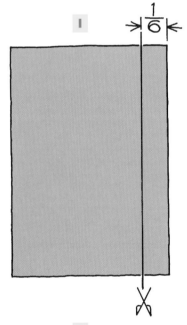

4. Fold over along the centre crease.

5. Fold in the top corners.

6. Create thin triangles as shown, tucking the centre corners up inside the thick nose layers, to lock the paper flat.

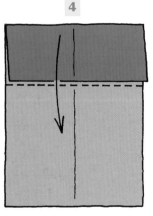

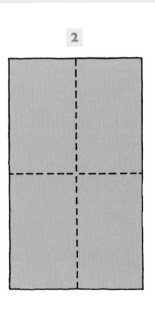

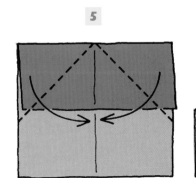

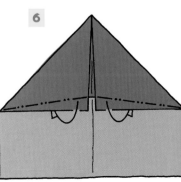

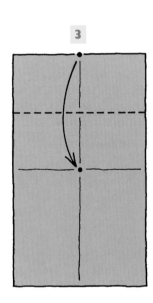

7. Mountain fold the paper in half.

8. Fold down the top pair of dots to lie on top of the bottom pair. Unfold. Repeat behind.

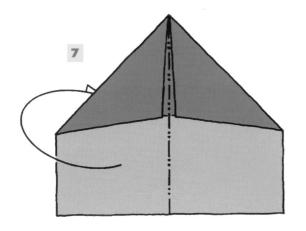

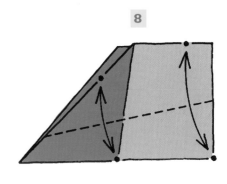

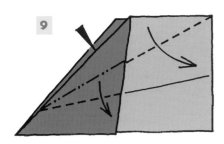

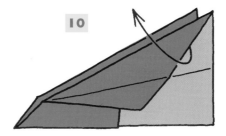

9. Squash fold as shown (see "Folding Techniques" p. 19), creating a new crease which extends to the top right-hand corner of the paper. Repeat behind.

10. Unfold the Squash. Repeat behind.

11. Adjust the Squash fold pockets to look like the profile shown here.

12. The Higby is complete.

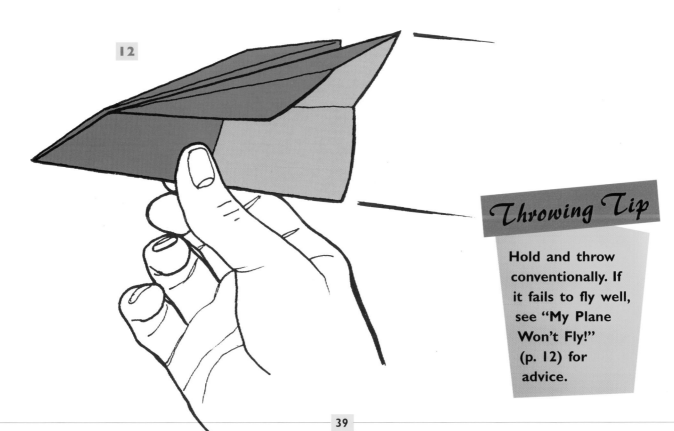

Throwing Tip

Hold and throw conventionally. If it fails to fly well, see "My Plane Won't Fly!" (p. 12) for advice.

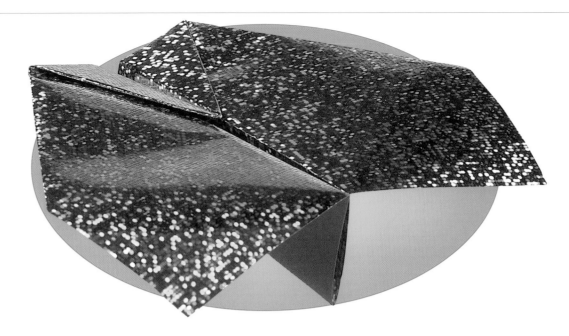

Lock-nosed Plane

Note how the Reverse fold in Step 7 and the accurately located wing crease in Step 9 lock the nose shut, so that the fuselage cannot open during flight.   *Designed by Yoshihide Momotani, Japan.*

Use a 15–20cm (6–8in) square of paper.

1

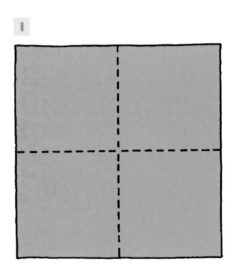

1. Fold a square in half, horizontally and vertically. Unfold both creases.

2

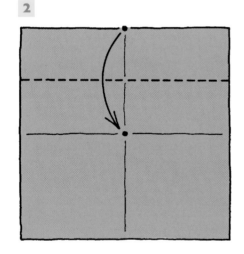

2. Fold the top edge to the centre.

3

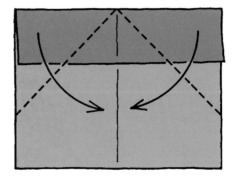

3. Fold the top corners to the centre crease.

4

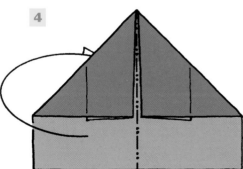

4. Mountain fold the paper in half.

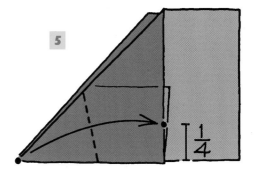

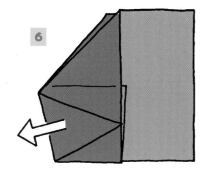

5. Fold the nose to an imaginary point, one-quarter of the way up the vertical edge.

6. Unfold.

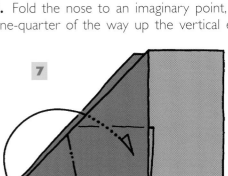

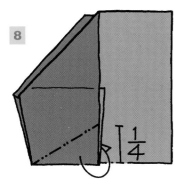

7. Inside Reverse fold the nose between the wings (see "Folding Techniques", p. 19).

8. Tuck the loose corner out of sight. Repeat behind.

9. Fold down the wings. Note how each crease touches the reversed nose point and how each crease slopes gently towards the front.

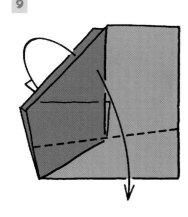

10. The Lock-nosed Plane is complete.

Throwing Tip

Hold and throw conventionally. If it fails to fly well, see "My Plane Won't Fly!" (p. 12) for advice.

Bill Glider

Remarkably simple, this reliable flier is a more elementary version of the "Hanging Hawk" (see p. 34) and the "Scooter" (see p. 32). Can you create a plane with fewer than five creases, the number used here?   *Designed by Earle Oakes, USA.*

Use A4 paper or a crisp dollar bill.

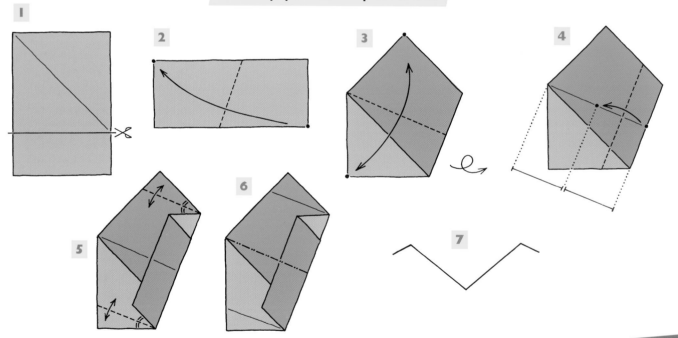

1. If you are not using a dollar bill, trim a square off an A4 or 1:√2 rectangle. Keep the rectangle, discarding the square.

2. Fold the bottom right-hand corner up to the top left-hand corner.

3. Fold in half dot to dot. Unfold.

4. Fold dot to dot.

5. Fold in the sides to lie against the short internal edges. Unfold.

6. Create a mountain fold down the centre.

7. Adjust the creases so that the Glider has this profile.

8. The Bill Glider is complete.

Throwing Tip

To launch, place your first finger on top of the centre crease, then point the Glider 45° downward and release. Don't release the Glider when it is horizontal and don't throw it.

Advanced Designs

An advanced model is not somehow "better" than the simple ones in the preceding chapter, or more worthy or more clever – it is merely more complicated to make. With a greater number of creases and the introduction of advanced folding techniques, the vocabulary of possible forms increases greatly and so the designs become more spectacular, adding to the entertainment value of making and flying paper planes.

Immamura Special

The shape of the Special is conventional, but the complex folding to achieve it creates a craft that is exquisitely balanced, so that it glides beautifully and with great reliability.   *Designed by Paolo Immamura, Brazil.*

Use a 15–20cm (6–8in) square paper.

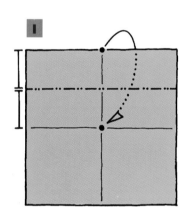

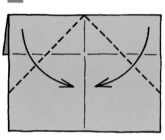

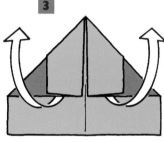

1. Crease and unfold horizontal and vertical folds. Mountain fold the top edge behind to touch the centre crease.

2. Fold in the top corners.

3. Unfold everything.

4. Collapse the creases as shown to create the Step 5 shape . . .

5. . . . like this. Fold the top section on the left across to the right.

6. Fold the top layer back to the centre crease.

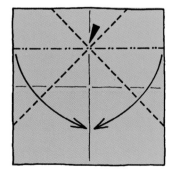

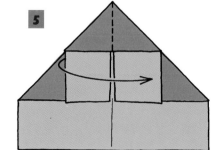

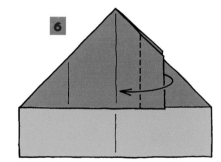

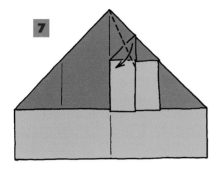

7. Fold the top sloping edge in to the centre crease.

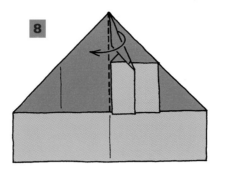

8. Return the newly-folded layers to the left.

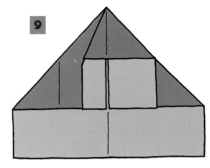

9. Repeat Steps 5–8 with the right-hand side.

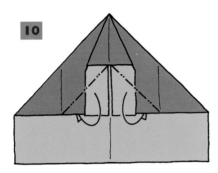

10. With mountain folds, accurately tuck the loose corners out of sight (it may be easier to crease them as valleys first).

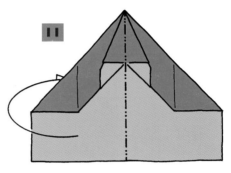

11. Mountain fold the paper in half.

12. Create a wing crease that begins at the nose and follows the hidden thick edge of the triangle, continuing to the trailing edge of the wing. Repeat behind.

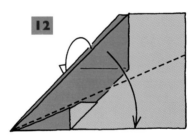

13. The Immamura Special is complete.

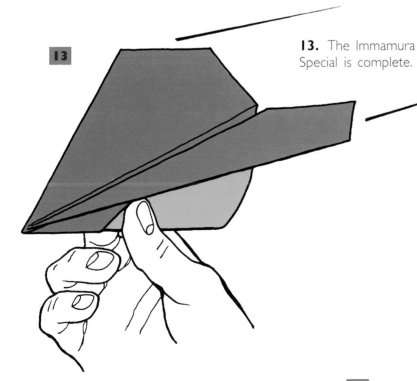

Throwing Tip

Hold and throw conventionally. If it fails to fly well, see "My Plane Won't Fly!" (p. 12) for advice.

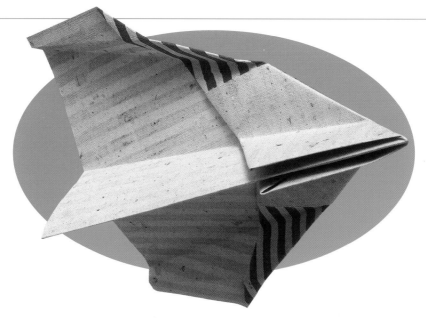

Lock Dart

The ingenious use of an Inside Reverse fold in Steps 8–10 and well-designed rudder creases in Steps 3–7, create a beautifully balanced, stable craft that is both interesting to fold and a joy to fly.   *Designed by Michael LaFosse, USA.*

Use a square of paper.

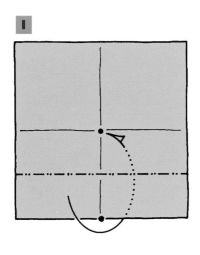

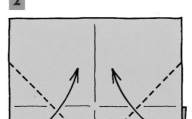

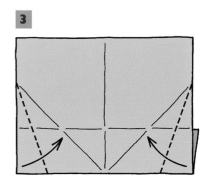

1. Crease and unfold horizontal and vertical centre folds, then mountain fold the bottom edge behind to touch the centre crease.

2. Fold in the bottom corners. Unfold.

3. Fold in the bottom corners to the unfolded creases, as shown.

4. Fold over along the Step 2 creases.

5. Fold dot to dot, bringing the sloping edge to lie alongside the short internal vertical edge.

6. Fold the inner dots to lie on top of the outer dots.

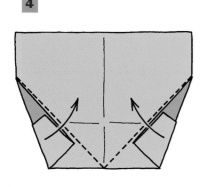

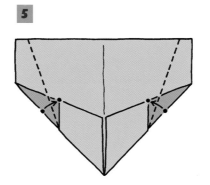

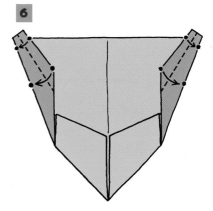

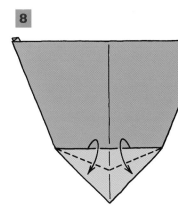

7. Turn over.

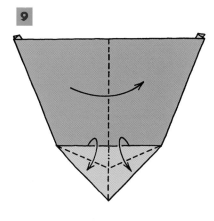

8. Create two valley folds on the top layer only.

9. Fold the paper in half, also folding the Step 8 creases ...

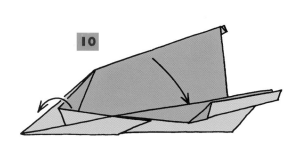

10. ... like this. Notice how the 'V'-shape is collapsing inside the nose.

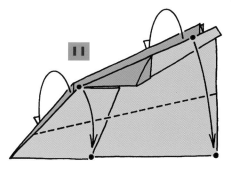

11. Fold down the upper dots to lie on top of the lower dots. Repeat behind. Pull open the pleated rudders.

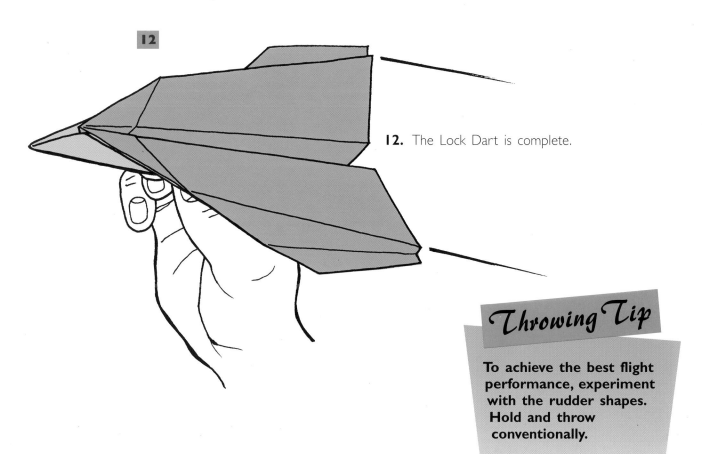

12. The Lock Dart is complete.

Throwing Tip

To achieve the best flight performance, experiment with the rudder shapes. Hold and throw conventionally.

Chuck Finn

The bulking of the layers towards the nose up to Step 8 means that the rudders created in Step 8 will curve instead of rising straight and flat. Don't panic! The curving actually aids stability.   *Designed by Michael LaFosse, USA.*

Use a 15–20cm (6–8in) square of paper.

1

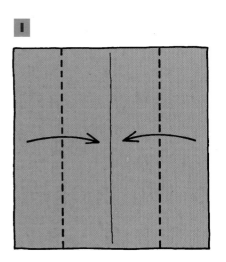

2

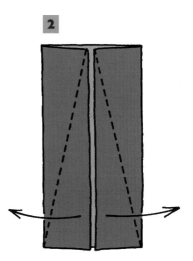

3

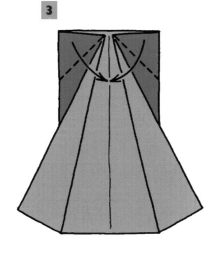

4

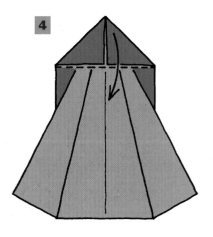

1. Crease and unfold a vertical centre crease. Fold the sides to the centre.

2. Fold out the loose bottom corners along diagonals, as shown. Be accurate.

3. Fold in the top corners.

4. Fold down the top point.

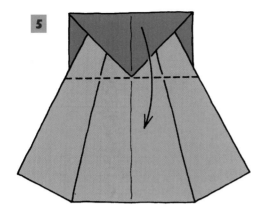

5. Fold down the top edge along a crease that touches what was the top point in Step 4.

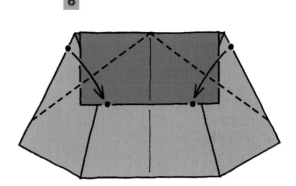

6. Fold dot to dot, as shown.

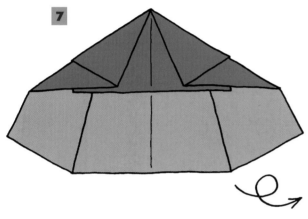

7. Turn over.

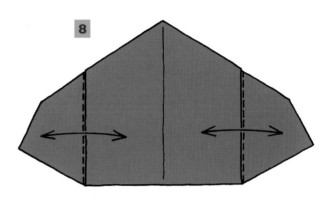

8. Make vertical valley folds, as shown.

9. The Chuck Finn is complete.

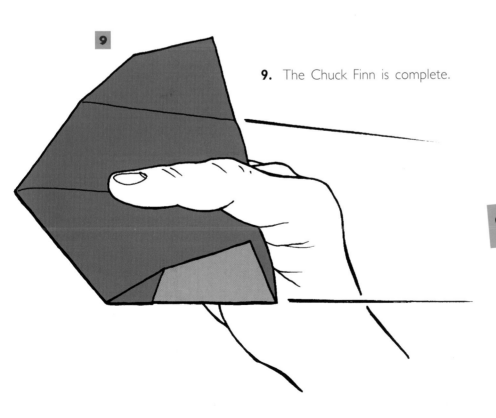

Throwing Tip

To launch, place your first finger on top of the central crease and throw horizontally forwards with a smooth flick.

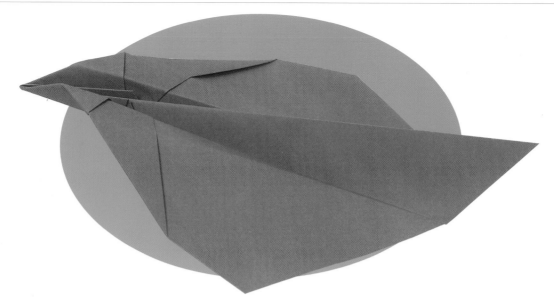

Stunt Plane

The creator is known for his Pureland designs: that is, designs made from valley/mountain folds only. The conventional way to create a tailplane is to reverse the fuselage upwards, but here, the same shape is created with an ingenious Pureland pleat at Step 9.   *Designed by John Smith, UK.*

Use a 15–20cm (6–8in) square of thin paper.

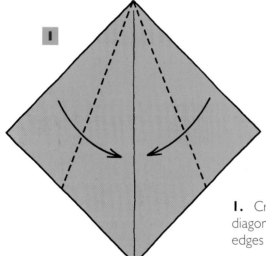

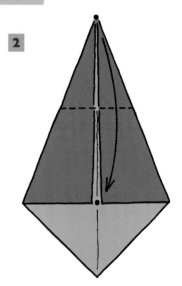

1. Crease and unfold a diagonal, then bring the top edges to the centre crease.

2. Fold dot to dot.

3. Turn over.

4. Fold in the top corners.

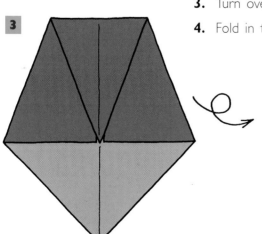

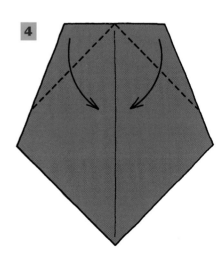

50

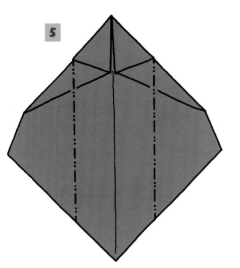

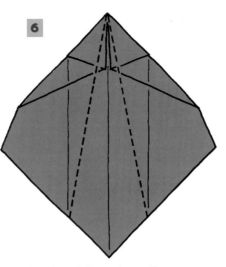

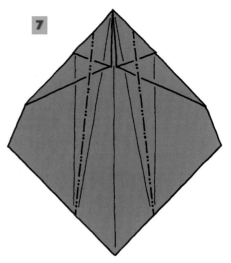

5. Make mountain creases parallel to the centre line. Note where the creases end at the top.

6. Carefully make valley creases which begin at the nose and end at the bottom of the mountains. Be accurate.

7. Now make mountain creases midway between the existing valley and mountain creases. Again, be accurate.

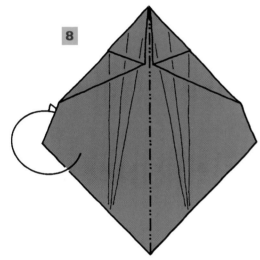

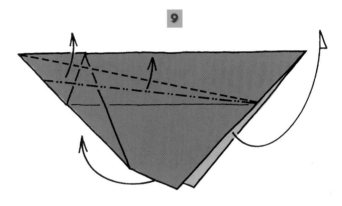

8. Mountain fold the paper in half.

9. To lift the wing, re-fold the valley and upper mountain creases. Repeat behind.

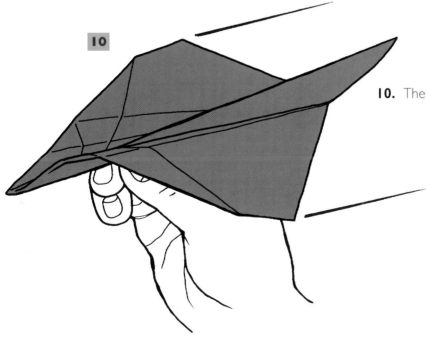

10. The Stunt Plane is complete.

Throwing Tip

Try holding, launching and trimming it in a variety of ways to achieve long glides, loops, circular flights and acrobatics.

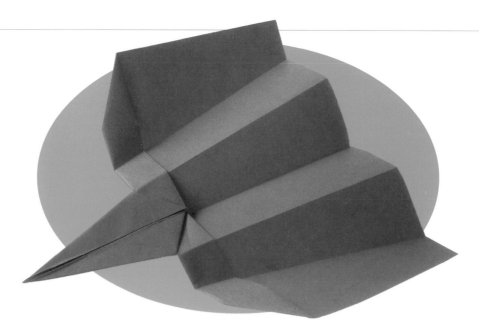

Needle Floater

The very thin nose on this design needs folding with great care and with some strength at Step 10. Folded well, the craft becomes an excellent flier and is an elegant sight in the air.   *Designed by Nick Robinson, UK.*

Use A4 or 8¹/₂ x 11in paper trimmed to a 1:√2 rectangle.

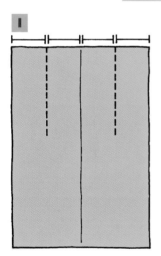

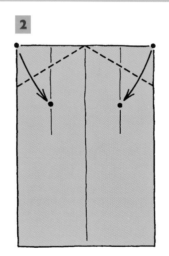

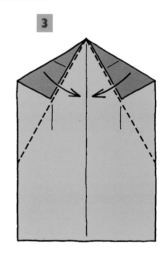

1. Fold and unfold a vertical centre crease. Crease quarter creases that end midway down the sheet.

2. Fold in the top corners to the quarter creases, so that both new creases begin exactly in the middle of the top edge.

3. Fold in the triangles to the centre crease.

4. Fold in the sloping edges to the centre, then unfold.

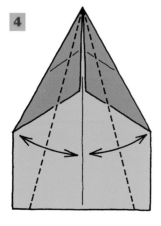

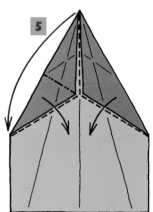

5. Make valley folds along the bottom edges of the thick triangles. Then make three valley folds simultaneously, as shown, folding the nose in half and lifting it so that it points upwards. Flatten the nose back down so that it points to the left.

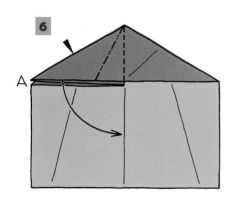

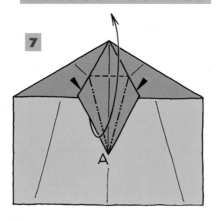

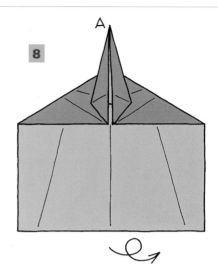

6. Lift up corner A (the nose) and Squash fold it flat (see "Folding Techniques", p. 19).

7. Use the mountain creases made at the nose in Step 4 to swing point A upwards through 180°, to create a long, thin forward-pointing nose. Add a short horizontal valley to assist the swing and note how the point narrows . . .

8. . . . like this. Turn over.

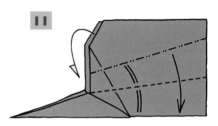

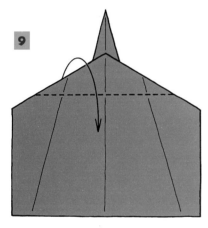

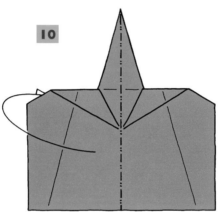

9. Pull down the blunt corner as far as it will go.

10. Mountain fold the paper in half.

11. The mountain fold is an existing crease. Create the valley by lowering the mountain onto the bottom edge. Repeat behind.

12. Adjust the creases so that the Floater has this profile.

13. The Needle Floater is complete.

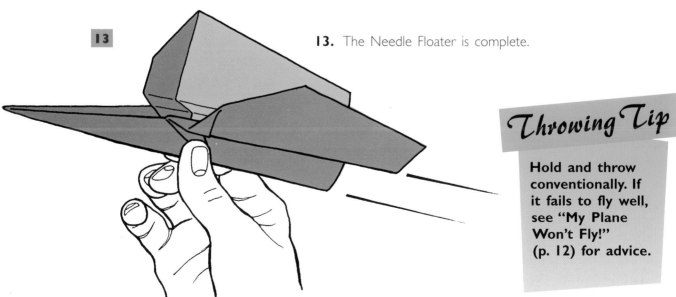

Throwing Tip

Hold and throw conventionally. If it fails to fly well, see "My Plane Won't Fly!" (p. 12) for advice.

The Cutter

Its flat, wide shape means that this design will slice through the air at a surprising speed, almost as though the launch was power-assisted.   *Designed by Paul Jackson, UK.*

Use a 20cm or 8in square of paper.

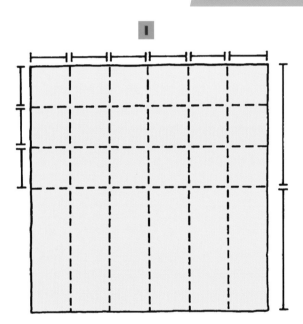

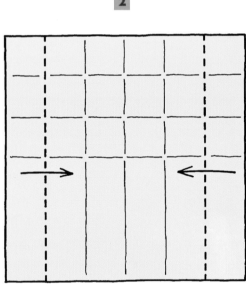

1. Divide a square into vertical sixths. Find the horizontal centre crease and divide the top half into thirds. If this is awkward, divide a square into easy eighths, then trim off two-eighths along adjacent edges to create sixths.

2. Fold in the left and right edges along the first crease.

3. Turn in the top corners.

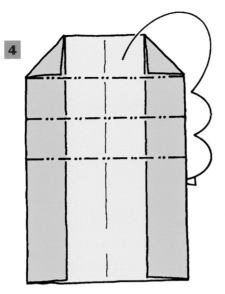

4. Roll the top edge behind, along three mountain folds.

5. Fold out the loose corners, as shown.

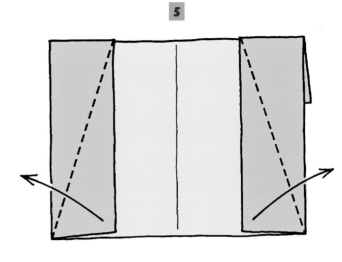

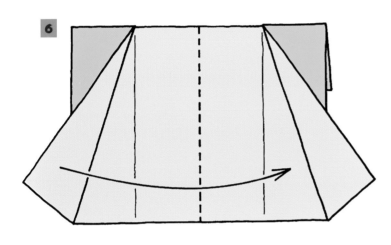

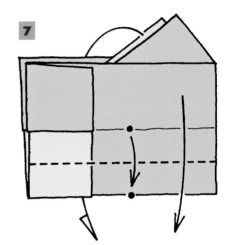

6. Valley fold the paper in half.

7. Carefully fold dot to dot, creating a crease parallel to the bottom edge. Repeat behind.

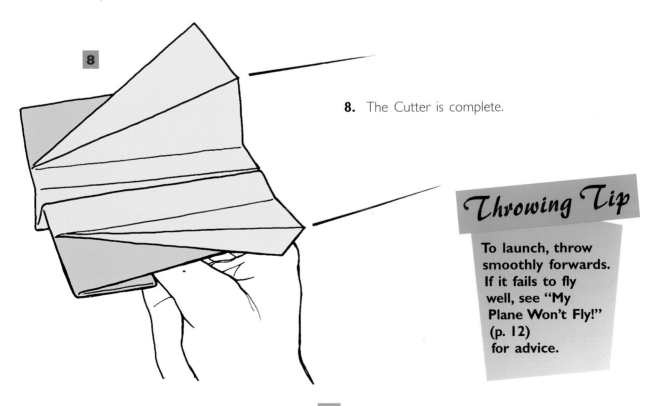

8. The Cutter is complete.

Throwing Tip

To launch, throw smoothly forwards. If it fails to fly well, see "My Plane Won't Fly!" (p. 12) for advice.

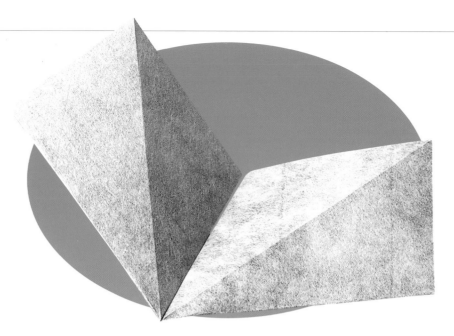

Stealth Wing

The critical step here is Step 2. Take as much time as you need to establish the creases with great accuracy, so that Step 4 is exactly symmetrical. From there, the design still needs folding carefully.   *Designed by Paul Jackson, UK.*

Use a 20cm (8in) square of paper.

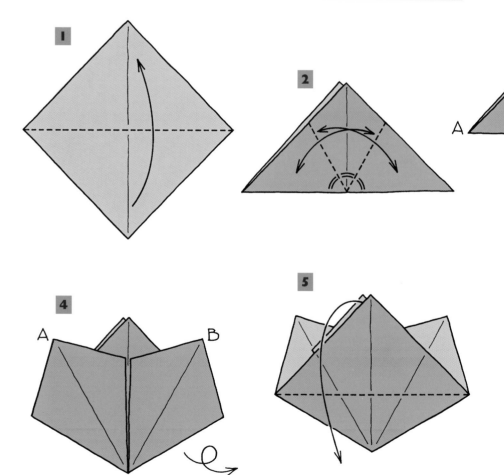

1. Crease and unfold the vertical diagonal, then fold the horizontal diagonal.

2. With two valley folds, create three equal angles, as shown. This can take a little time, so don't crease heavily until you are sure that they are accurately located. Unfold.

3. Using the valleys as guides, create Squash folds (see "Folding Techniques" p. 19). Note A & B.

4. Turn over.

5. Pull down the upper layer as far as it will go.

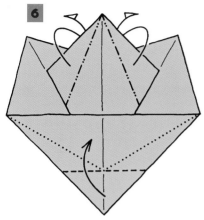

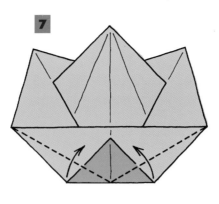

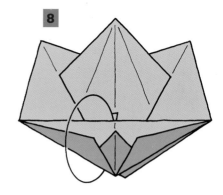

6. Fold up the bottom corner so that the crease lines up with the corner beneath. With mountain folds, narrow the top corner, then unfold.

7. Fold in the bottom corners.

8. Swing the top layer back on itself, so that it tucks neatly into the pocket behind.

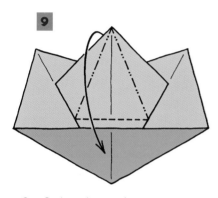

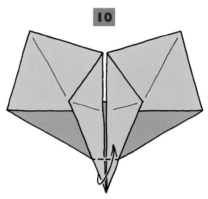

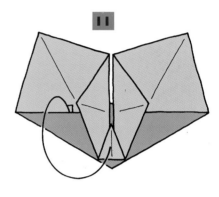

9. Swing down the top corner using the mountain folds made in Step 6, adding a horizontal valley to assist the swing. Look at Step 10 to see the result.

10. Fold up the bottom point so that it does not project beyond the edges beneath.

11. Tuck the same point into the pocket beneath. No new creases are made.

12. Create a shallow mountain crease down the centre. Turn over.

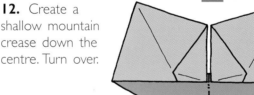

13. The Stealth Wing is complete.

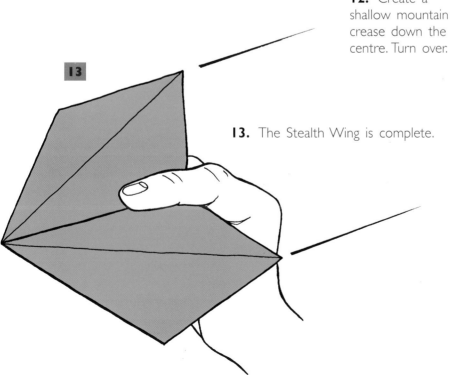

Throwing Tip

To launch, place your first finger on top of the centre crease and throw forwards with a smooth flick.

Glynn's Glider

This remarkable design presently holds the official Guinness Book of Records World Record of 28.7m (94ft) in the Origami Distance category, set by its designer at the Yorkshire Air Museum, Yorkshire, England, on 19th September 1997. Other paper planes have flown further, but none were pure origami (folded from a rectangle without cuts and without the aid of glue, tape, weights, etc.).   *Designed by Robin Glynn, UK.*

Use A4 paper or 8½ x 11in paper trimmed to a 1:√2 rectangle.

1

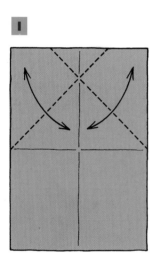

2

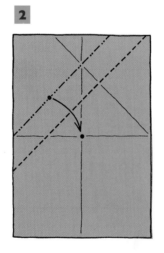

3

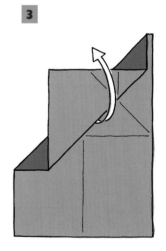

4

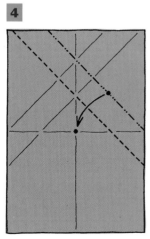

5

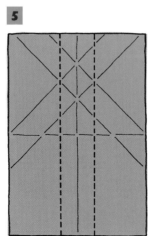

1. Crease and unfold horizontal and vertical centre folds. Crease and unfold 45° diagonals on the top half, as shown. Turn over.

2. Fold dot to dot, bringing the existing mountain diagonal crease to the centre point and flattening to create a new valley crease, parallel to the mountain . . .

3. . . . like this. Unfold.

4. Repeat Step 2 on the right.

5. Create vertical valleys which touch the corners of the small, creased diamond near the top edge. Be accurate.

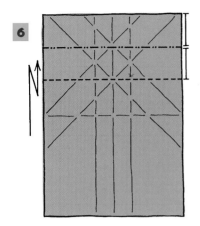

6. Create a horizontal valley which touches the bottom corner of the same creased diamond, then a mountain, midway between the valley and the top edge.

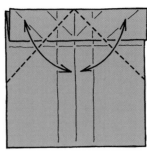

7. Fold in the top corners. Unfold.

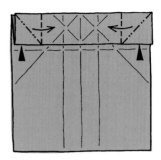

8. Create Squash folds (see "Folding Techniques" p. 19), swinging the single thickness top corners towards the centre.

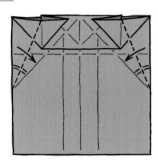

9. Fold in the top corners to lie along the Step 7 creases.

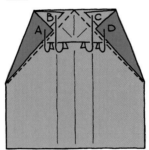

10. Re-fold the Step 7 creases, tucking corners A & B and corners C & D under the horizontal edge. This locks the paper flat.

11. Re-form the vertical valleys and make a central mountain crease.

12. Add a rudder to the wing. Repeat behind.

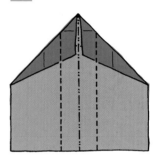

13. Glynn's Glider is complete.

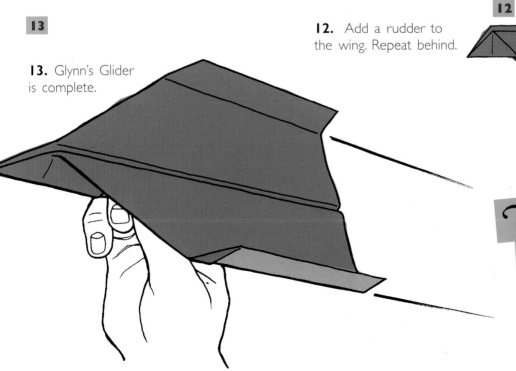

Throwing Tip

Hold and throw conventionally. With only minimal adjustments to the angles of the wings and rudders, it should fly a great distance.

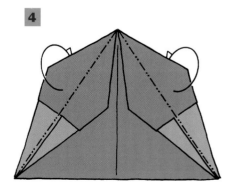

Thunder Bomber

This is one of those very pleasing designs that seems to fold itself. The sequence is somehow "obvious" and flowing, with no awkward contrivances. It flies superbly, too. *Traditional.*

Use A4 paper or 8½ x 11in paper trimmed to a 1:√2 rectangle.

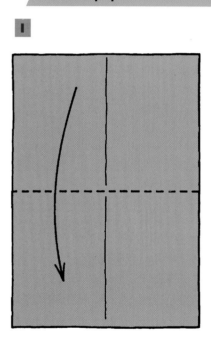

1

2

1. Crease and unfold down the centre, then fold the top edge down to the bottom edge.

2. Create two Squash folds (see "Folding Techniques", p. 19). Note the positioning of the valley folds.

3. With mountain folds, narrow the open ends of the Squash folds.

4. Fold the Squash folds in half. The paper will then be the same, front and back.

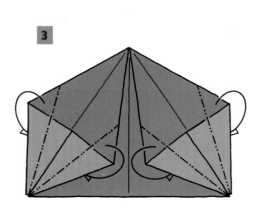

3

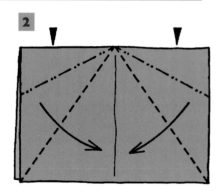

4

5

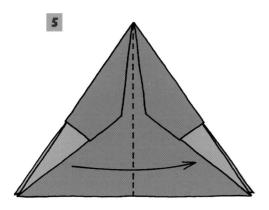

5. Valley fold the paper in half.

6

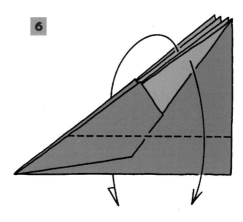

6. Valley fold the wing downward. Repeat behind.

7

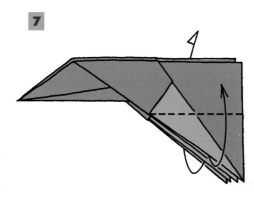

7. Fold the top layer of the wing upwards. Repeat behind.

8

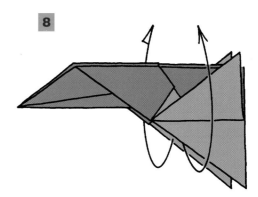

8. Lift the wings to the horizontal.

9

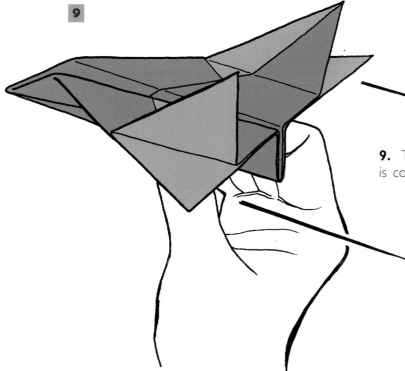

9. The Thunder Bomber is complete.

Throwing Tip

Hold and throw conventionally. If it fails to fly well, see "My Plane Won't Fly!" (p. 12) for advice.

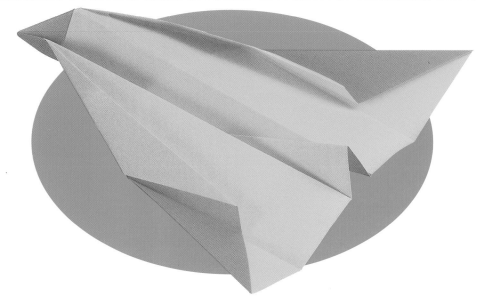

Classique

This design has a familiar delta shape, but the careful selection of a proportion in the Step 1 creases creates just the right amount of weight in the nose to balance the craft in flight.
Designed by Alain Georgeot and Eric Joisel, France.

Use a 20cm (8in) square paper.

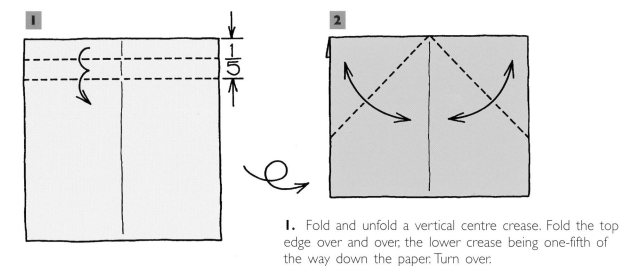

1. Fold and unfold a vertical centre crease. Fold the top edge over and over, the lower crease being one-fifth of the way down the paper. Turn over.

2. Fold in the top corners. Unfold.

3. Fold in the sides to lie along the existing creases.

4. Fold over along the Step 2 creases.

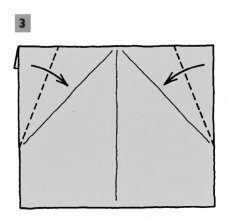

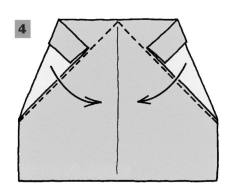

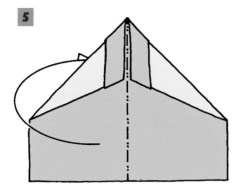

5. Mountain fold the paper in half.

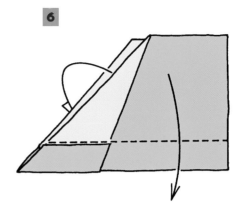

6. Fold down the wing. Repeat behind.

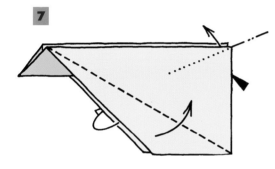

7. Reverse out a tail plane. Fold in the leading edge of the wing. Repeat behind.

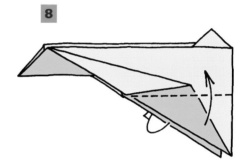

8. Fold up the wing tip. Repeat behind.

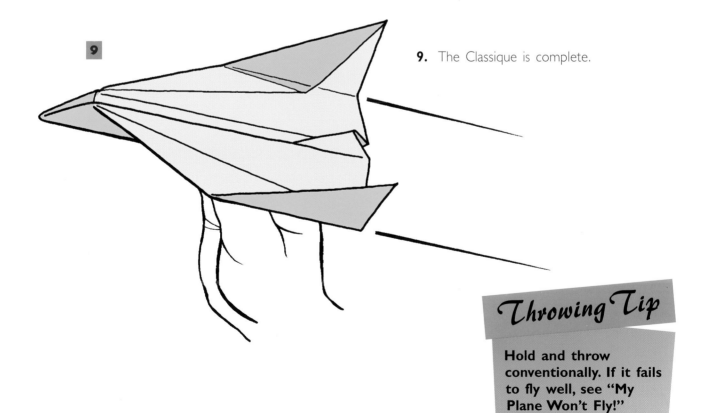

9. The Classique is complete.

Throwing Tip

Hold and throw conventionally. If it fails to fly well, see "My Plane Won't Fly!" (p. 12) for advice.

Launch Assist

The shape of the plane is conventional, but the addition of the spike means that it can be thrown with great force. The angle of dihedral remains the same after launch, so that the plane is immediately aerodynamic and will fly. *Designed by Paul Jackson, UK.*

Use a 15–20cm (6–8in) square paper.

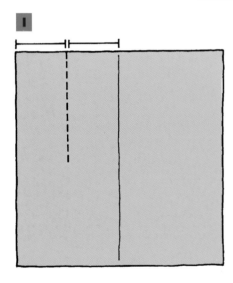

1. Crease and unfold down the centre. Fold the left-hand quarter crease, but not all the way down to the bottom edge.

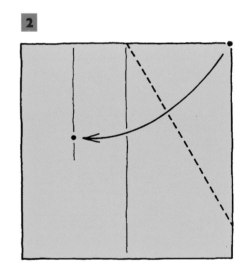

2. Fold the top right-hand corner across, so that it lies on the quarter crease in such a way that the new crease begins exactly in the middle of the top edge. Be accurate.

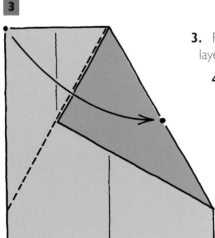

3. Fold dot to dot. The left-hand and right-hand layers should all line up exactly.

4. Crease and unfold. Note the position of the crease.

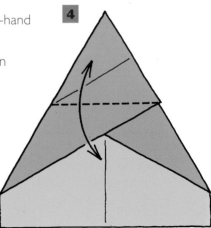

5

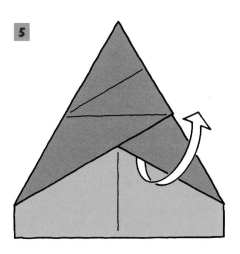

5. Unfold.

6

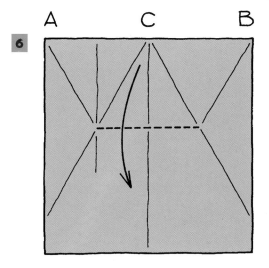

6. Crease *only* the short horizontal section shown . . .

7

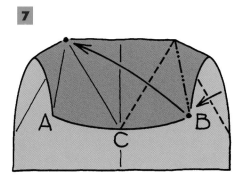

7. . . . like this. Fold corner B up to the top left corner, flattening the right-hand side of the paper.

8

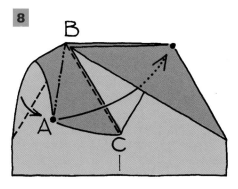

8. Repeat on the other side with A. Note how A tucks right underneath the top layer to lock the paper flat.

9

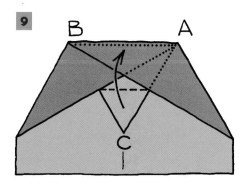

9. Fold up corner C.

10

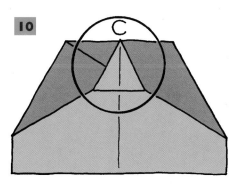

10. The next drawing enlarges C.

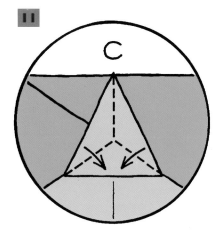

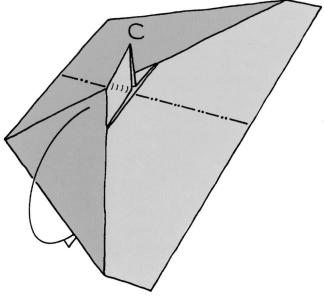

11. On the triangle below C, make three separate creases, one into each corner, then re-fold the lower pair.

12. This creates a 3-D spike at C. Mountain fold the paper in half.

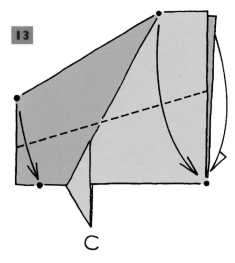

13. Note C. Fold the upper pair of dots down to the lower pair. Repeat behind.

14. The Launch Assist is complete.

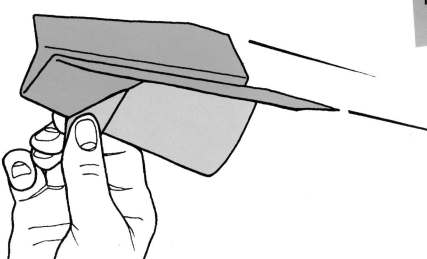

Throwing Tip

To launch, hold the spike firmly and throw high into the air. If it fails to fly well, see "My Plane Won't Fly!" (p. 12) for advice.

Unusual Designs

"Will *that* fly!" is the incredulous response to a design that is apparently as un-aerodynamic as a house brick, but which – magically – can still remain aloft. This chapter then, is the refuge for the odd, the unlikely, the unexpected and the bizarre. Included too are a few spinners, which, while not strictly planes, will often remain aloft longer than a conventional plane. So, suspend disbelief and enjoy.

Swan

This is one of those rare designs which seems obvious when seen, but which is actually very creative – would *you* have thought of it? It is little more than the traditional paper dart that we all learnt as children, but with the additional Reverse fold at Step 5. The result is dramatically different. *Designed by Yoshihide Momotani, Japan.*

Use a 15–20 (6–8in) square paper.

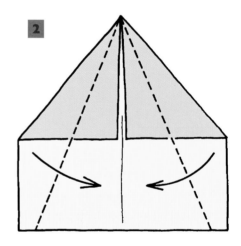

1. Crease and unfold down the centre, then fold in the top corners.

2. Bring the sloping edges to the centre crease.

3. Valley fold in half.

4. Crease and unfold the wing. Repeat behind. Note that the creases go exactly to the nose.

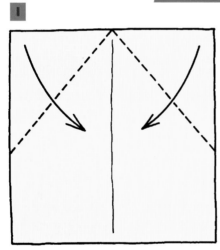

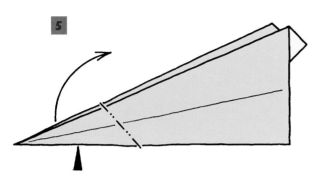

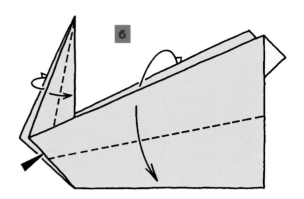

5. Reverse fold the nose (see "Folding Techniques" p. 19). Note that the bottom end of the crease is just in front of the mid-point of the bottom edge.

6. Re-fold the Step 4 creases, forming the wings and narrowing the neck.

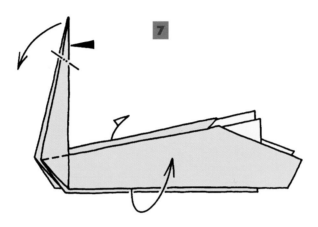

7. Reverse fold the head. Lift up the wings.

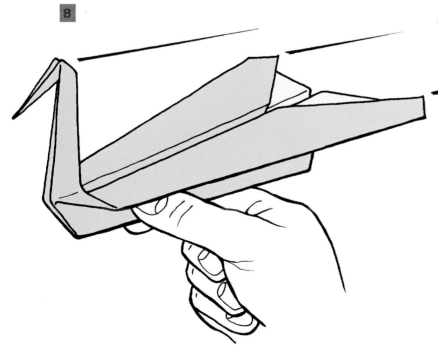

8. The Swan is complete.

Throwing Tip

Hold and throw conventionally. If it fails to fly well, see "My Plane Won't Fly!" (p. 12) for advice.

Butterfly

The key to folding this design successfully is in Step 1: take your time to make AB twice CD. With practice, the completed Butterfly will not only glide, but will flutter like a real butterfly. *Designed by Paul Jackson, UK.*

Use a 7.5–15cm (3–6in) square of thin paper for a fluttering effect and larger, heavier squares for the glide.

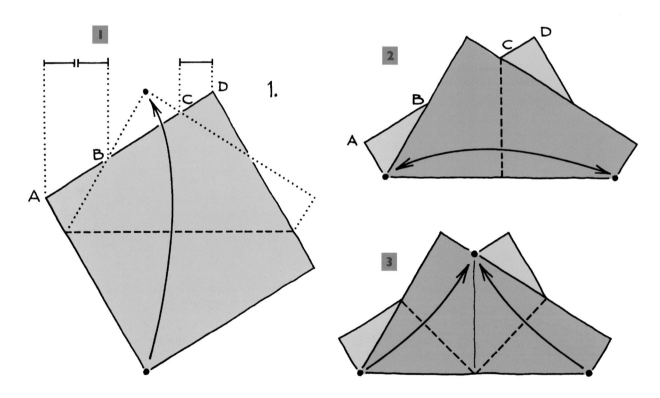

1. Fold the bottom corner up to the dotted position, in such a way that AB is twice CD. Take your time. Look at Step 2. Note that the outline of the paper will be symmetrical.

2. Fold in half, dot to dot.

3. Fold the bottom corners up to the central dot.

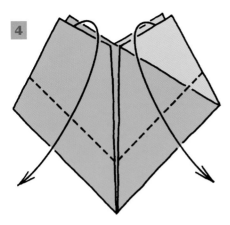

4. Pull down the top layer only, left and right. Look at Step 5 to see the exact shape you are trying to achieve.

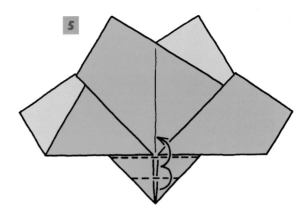

5. Fold the bottom corner up to the horizontal edge, then fold up again, level with the edge.

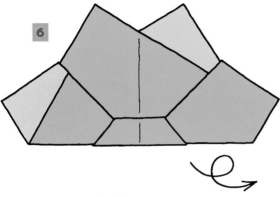

6. Turn over.

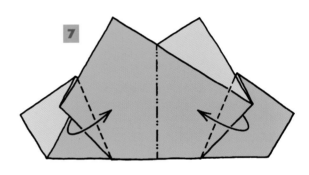

7. Fold the loose corners inward. Create a shallow mountain crease down the centre. Turn over.

8. Adjust the creases so that the Butterfly has this profile.

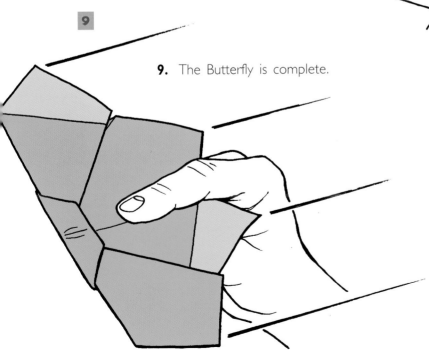

9. The Butterfly is complete.

Throwing Tip

To launch, place your first finger on top of the central crease and throw forwards with a gentle flick.

Sachet Glider

Easier to make and easier to remember than its companion design, the Sachet Stunt Plane (see p. 74), this unusual glider is remarkably well-balanced in the air when one considers the unlikely source of the paper.   *Designed by Earle Oakes, USA.*

Use an uncrumpled tea bag sachet.

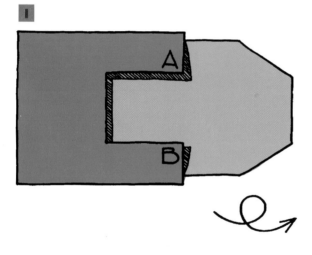

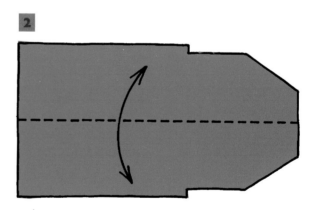

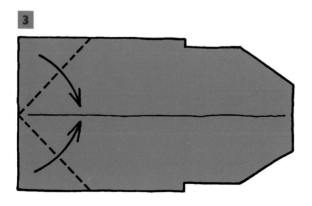

1. This is the pocket side of the sachet. Note A & B. Turn over.

2. Fold the centre crease. Unfold.

3. At the pocket end, fold in the corners.

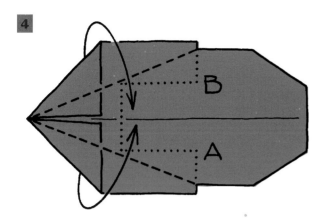

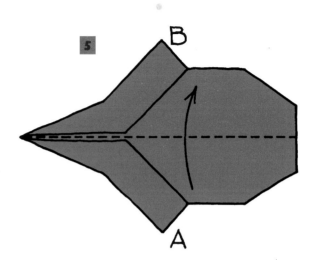

4. Narrow the nose again, but allow corners B & A to flip into view. Look at Step 5.

5. Fold in half.

6. Fold down the wing. Repeat behind. Inside Reverse fold the tail plane (see "Folding Techniques", p. 19).

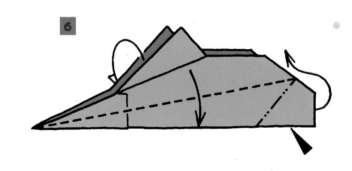

7. The Sachet Glider is complete.

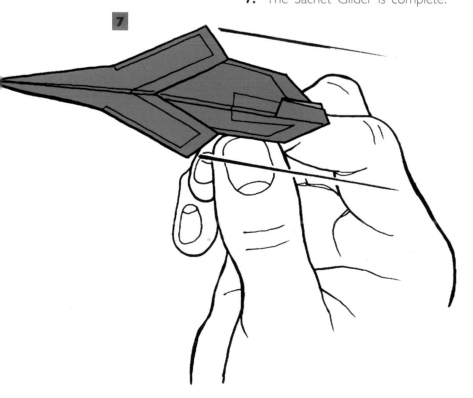

Throwing Tip

To launch, hold near the tail and throw smoothly forwards.

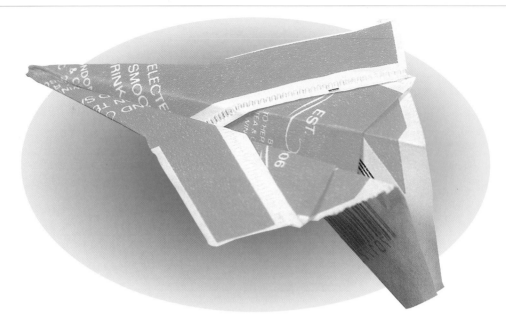

Sachet Stunt Plane

This fun design is ideal to make in a restaurant, at a party, at a meeting or at any social occasion that needs enlivening. With practice, it can be made to perform an amazingly wide repertoire of stunts.   *Designed by Earle Oakes, USA.*

Use an uncrumpled tea bag sachet.

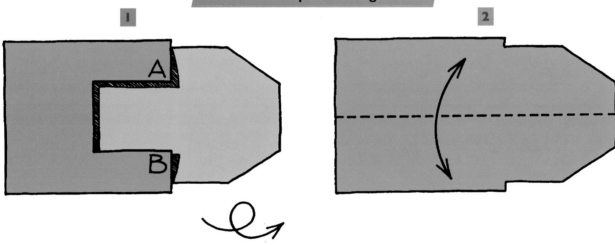

1. This is the pocket side of the sachet. Note A & B. Turn over.

2. Fold the centre crease. Unfold.

3. At the pocket end, fold in the corners.

4. Narrow the nose again, but allow corners B & A to flop into view. Look at Step 5.

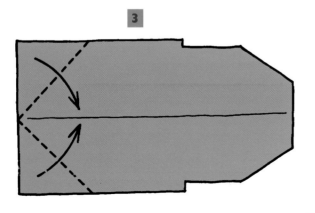

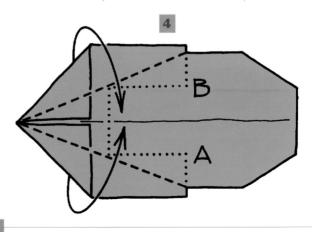

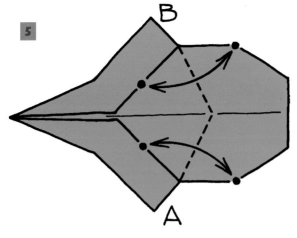

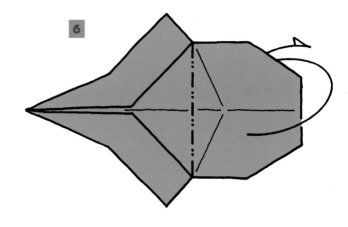

5. Fold dot to dot twice as shown, to create a shallow "V" across the centre.

6. Mountain fold where shown. Unfold.

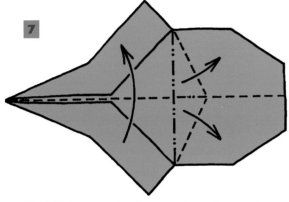

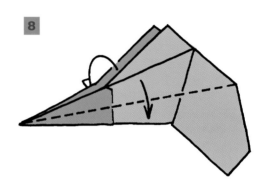

7. With care, simultaneously collapse all the creases until the Step 8 shape is achieved.

8. Make a wing crease that connects the tip of the nose with the rearmost corner of the plane. Repeat behind. Keep the point of the nose as neat as possible.

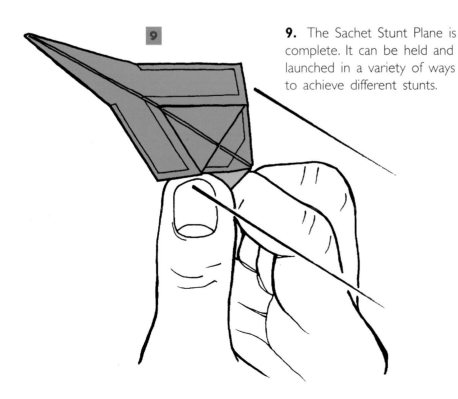

9. The Sachet Stunt Plane is complete. It can be held and launched in a variety of ways to achieve different stunts.

Throwing Tip

Try launching it horizontally, or holding the nose and throwing it to the side, or holding the nose and throwing it vertically with the tail plane facing you.

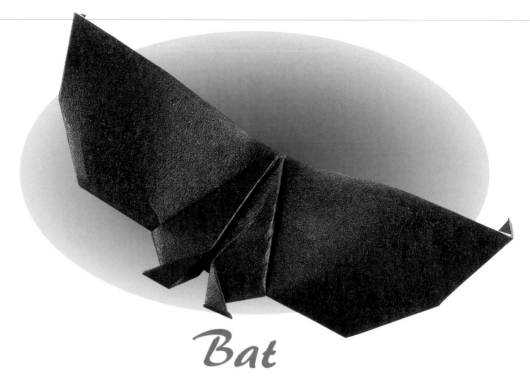

Bat

Designed in the early 1970s, when the creator was still a boy, the Bat is an effective variation on a well-known 2-piece plane, in which a long, narrow tail is pushed into a shape which resembles the Bat. *Designed by David Morgan, UK.*

Use a 15–20cm or 6–8in square of thin paper.

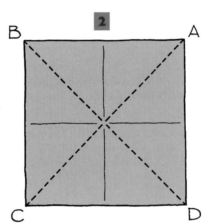

1. Fold the bottom edge up to the top edge. Unfold. Fold the left-hand edge across to the right-hand edge. Unfold. Turn over.

2. Crease a diagonal. Unfold. Crease the other diagonal. Unfold.

3. Collapse both diagonals and the horizontal mountain . . .

4. . . . like this. Notice how B & A move down to touch C & D. Fold B & A up to E.

5. Create three creases on the left and right triangles, then collapse them . .

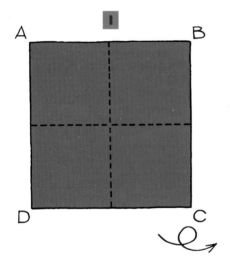

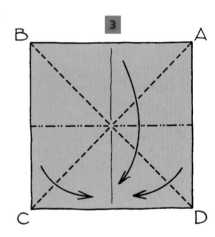

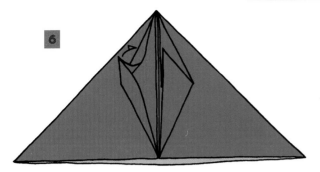

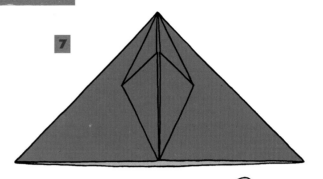

6. . . . like this, on the left. The loose corner should be flattened so that it points upwards, as shown on the right.

7. Turn over.

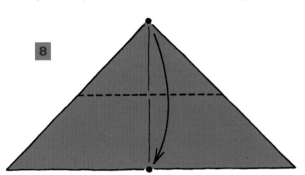

8. Fold dot to dot.

9. Outside Reverse fold the ears (see "Folding Techniques" p. 19). Valley fold the wing tips.

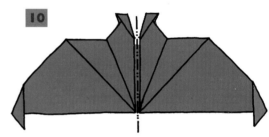

10. Make a shallow mountain crease down the centre. Turn over.

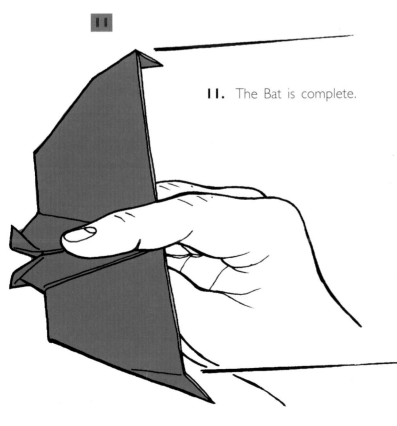

11. The Bat is complete.

Throwing Tip

To launch, place your first finger on top of the central crease and flick smoothly forwards.

Human Cannonball

A design as whimsical as this one ought not to fly at all, and in truth, it takes a little coaxing. The secret is to curl the trailing edges of the arms upwards to just the right angle, after which our brave hero will glide a surprising distance, even without a safety net! *Designed by Jean-Jerome Casalonga, France.*

Use a 20cm or 8in square of thin paper.

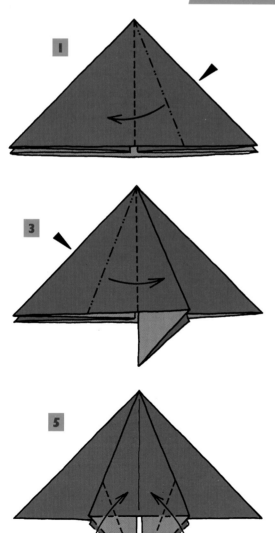

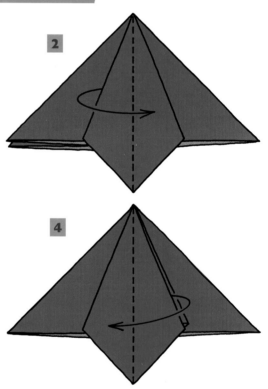

1. Begin with Step 4 of the Bat (see p. 76). Lift and Squash fold the front right-hand flap (see "Folding Techniques", p. 19).

2. Fold the Squash fold over to the right.

3. Repeat Step 2 on the left.

4. Repeat Step 3.

5. The paper is now symmetrical. Narrow the corners at the bottom, front layer only.

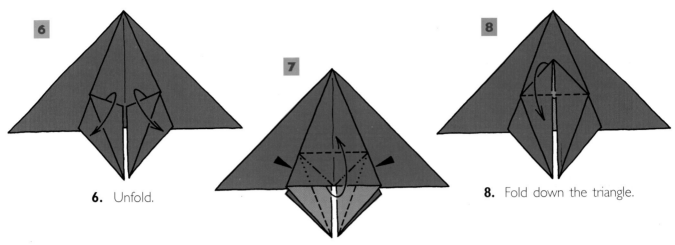

6. Unfold.

8. Fold down the triangle.

7. Lift the raw horizontal edge which crosses the middle. Allow the sides to collapse inward along the Step 5 creases. Flatten the paper to look like Step 8, swivelling the raw edge upwards. Note the horizontal valley and the two mountain creases.

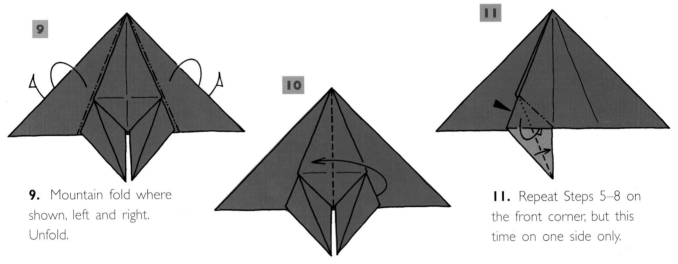

9. Mountain fold where shown, left and right. Unfold.

10. Fold the layers on the right across to the left, but leave the big triangle at the rear in position.

11. Repeat Steps 5–8 on the front corner, but this time on one side only.

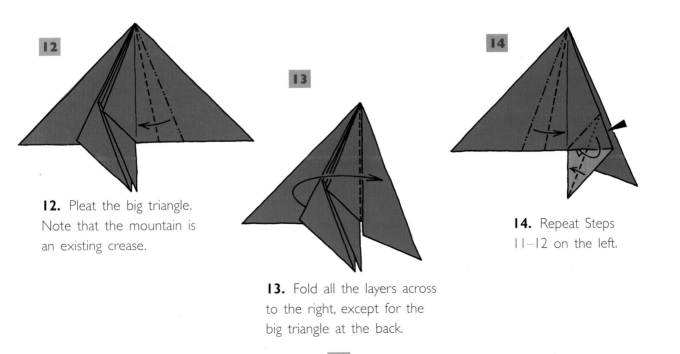

12. Pleat the big triangle. Note that the mountain is an existing crease.

13. Fold all the layers across to the right, except for the big triangle at the back.

14. Repeat Steps 11–12 on the left.

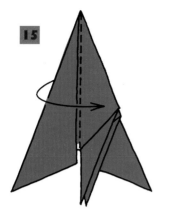

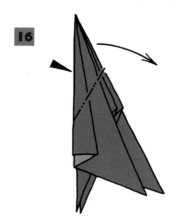

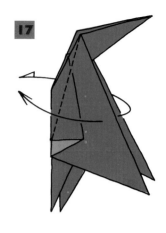

15. Fold all the remaining layers on the left across to the right.

16. Inside Reverse fold the top corner (see "Folding Techniques", p. 19). Note the exact position of the crease.

17. Pull back the arm as far as it will go. Repeat behind.

18. Reverse the feet. Pleat the face to create a nose.

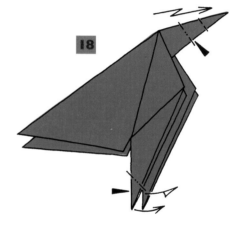

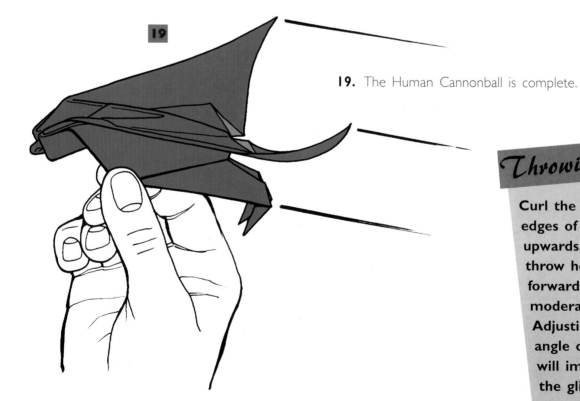

19. The Human Cannonball is complete.

Throwing Tip

Curl the trailing edges of the arms upwards. To launch, throw horizontally forwards at moderate speed. Adjusting the angle of curl will improve the glide.

Gliding Swan

Of all the designs in the book, this one is perhaps the most ungainly, yet it flies with great reliability if folded accurately.   *Designed by Paul Jackson, UK.*

Use a 20cm (8in) square of thin paper.

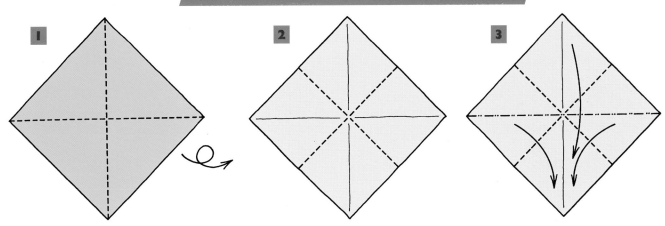

1. Crease a diagonal. Unfold. Crease the other diagonal. Unfold. Turn over.

2. Fold one edge across to the opposite edge. Unfold. Fold an adjacent edge across to the opposite edge. Unfold.

3. Collapse the two valleys and the horizontal mountain as shown.

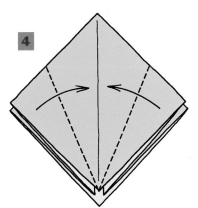

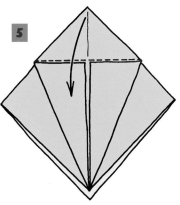

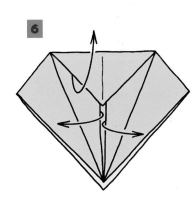

4. Note the open corner at the bottom. Fold in the lower edges of the top flaps, left and right …

5. … like this. Fold down the top corner.

6. Unfold the Step 4 and Step 5 creases.

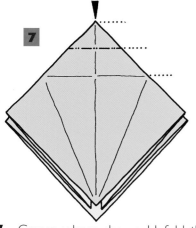

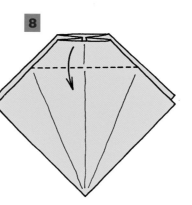

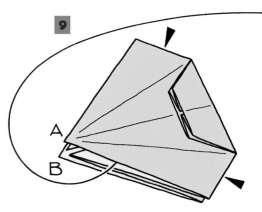

7. Crease where shown. Unfold the paper almost back to Step 3, then sink the top corner down inside the layers. This isn't easy, so take your time!

8. Re-fold the Step 5 crease.

9. Lift the single layers at A up into the air . . .

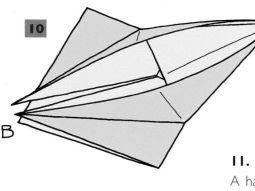

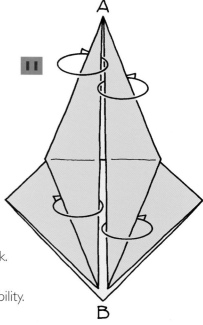

10. . . like this, pulling it over to the right. It will begin to fall flat, forming a narrow diamond shape . . .

11. . . like this. Notice how A has moved a considerable distance. Swing the top layer on the left and right around to the back. This is difficult and is best done by unfolding the paper to increase flexibility.

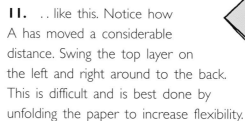

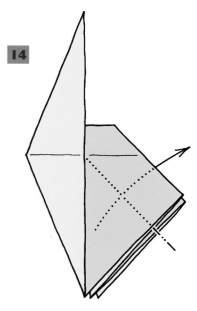

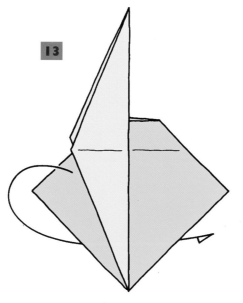

12. Fold the diamond in half.

13. Fold the left-hand section of the square round the back to the right.

14. Reverse fold out the middle point (see "Folding Techniques", p. 19). Look at Step 15 to see its exact location.

15

16

15. Narrow the top corner. Repeat behind.

16. Fold up the nearside wing. Note the exact position of the crease. Repeat behind.

17

18

19

18. Pleat the beak … **19.** … like this.

17. Reverse fold the head. Pleat the wing. Repeat behind. Note how the mountain crease meets the trailing edge of the wing at 90°.

20

20. Adjust the creases until the Swan has this profile.

21

21. The Gliding Swan is complete.

Throwing Tip

To launch, hold just behind the point of balance and throw gracefully forwards. If it fails to fly well, see "My Plane Won't Fly!" (p. 12) for advice.

Helicopter

This spinner is unusual because it is not dropped, but thrown high into the air to begin its descent, thus both increasing its entertainment value and prolonging its time aloft. *Designed by Robert Abes, USA.*

Use a 15–20cm (6–8in) square of paper.

1. Begin with Step 4 of the "Gliding Swan" (see p. 81). Rotate the paper so that the open corner is at the top. Fold down the top layer. Repeat behind.

2. Fold corner D across to lie on top of corners C & B. Fold B behind to lie behind corner A.

3. Fold A, B, C & D to the centre, so that all the creases go to the bottom point . . .

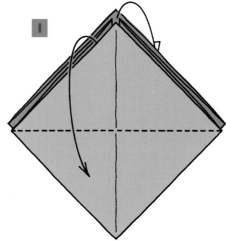

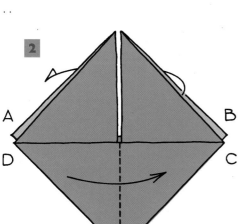

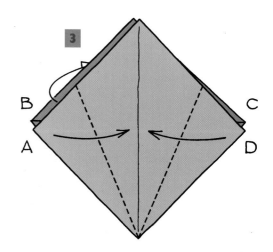

4. . . . like this. Fold A across to lie on top of D. Fold C behind to lie behind B. This undoes Step 2.

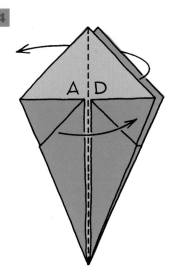

5. Fold the right-hand blade behind and the left-hand blade forwards. Crease firmly.

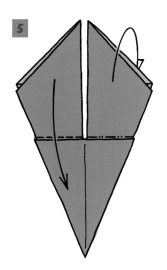

6. The Helicopter is complete.

Throwing Tip

To launch, hold the solid point and throw as hard as possible, high into the air. The blades spin best when they form a 'Y'-shape, not a 'T'.

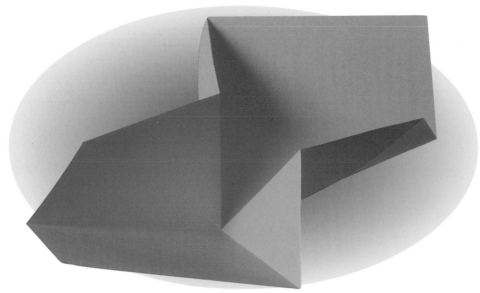

Twirly

Although easy to make, the drawings need to be followed with great care as it is surprisingly easy to lose one's sense of up, down, left and right.   *Designed by Nick Robinson, UK.*

Use a 7.5–20cm (3–8in) square paper.

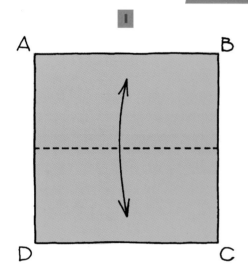

1. Fold across the centre. Unfold.

2. Fold corner C up to corner A. Unfold. Turn over.

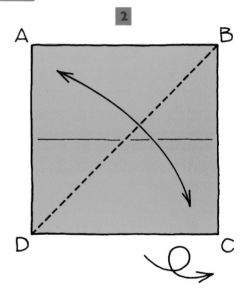

3. Fold corners B & D to the centre line.

4. Fold corner C to corner A. Unfold.

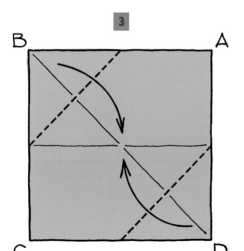

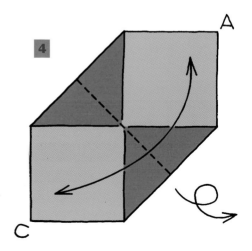

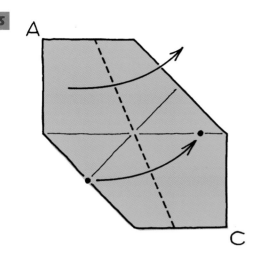

5. Fold dot to dot. Note how the new crease intersects with the others at the centre point. Look at Step 6 to see the result.

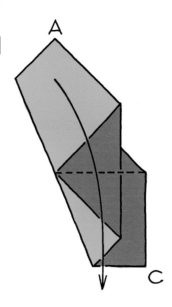

6. Fold A downward.

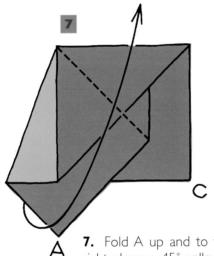

7. Fold A up and to the right along a 45° valley fold.

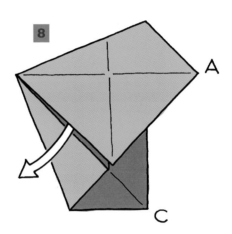

8. Pull open the layers to make a 3-D form.

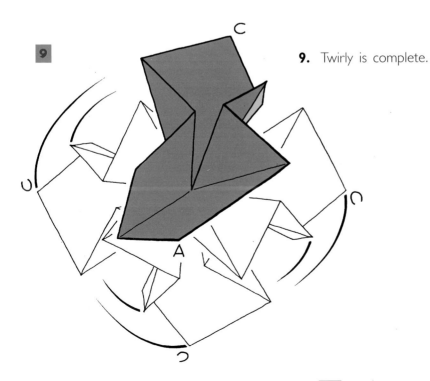

9. Twirly is complete.

Throwing Tip

To launch, hold high above your head and release, point down. As it descends, it will spin gracefully! Experiment with how open or closed the form should be to achieve the best rate of spin.

Sycamore Seed

There are many spinning sycamore seed designs, but this is the only one that can be folded from large sheets to increase the visual impact of the spin.   *Designed by John Smith, UK.*

Use a 1:√2 rectangle of any size, including very large rectangles 60–90cm (2–3ft) across.

1

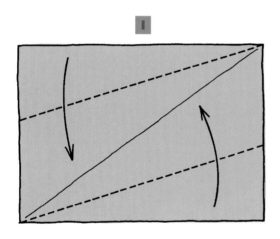

2

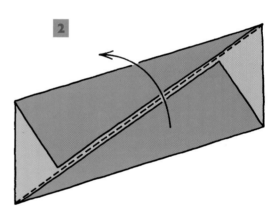

1. Begin by creasing a long diagonal. Unfold. This can be awkward, so take your time. Fold in the long edges to lie along the diagonal crease.

2. Fold in half along the existing diagonal crease.

3. At the left, fold down the triangle.

4. Tuck the excess behind.

5. Fold the top edge down behind. Note where the crease ends at the bottom left.

3

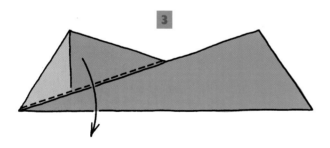

4

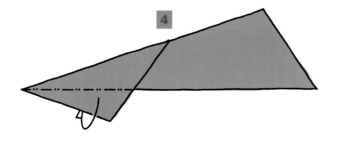

5

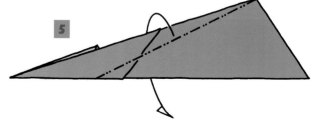

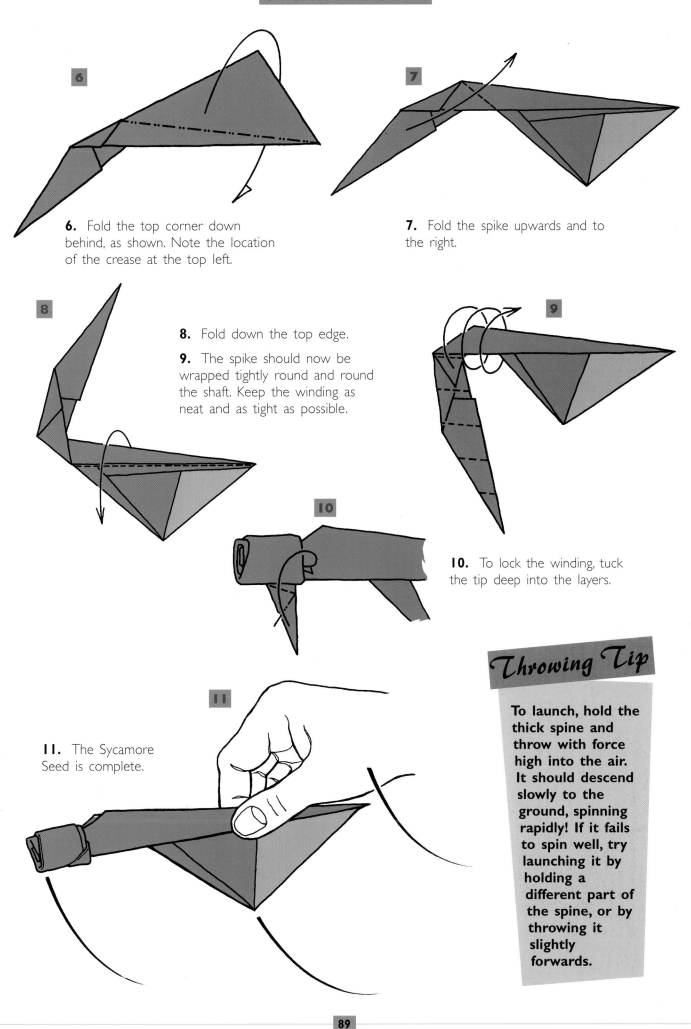

6. Fold the top corner down behind, as shown. Note the location of the crease at the top left.

7. Fold the spike upwards and to the right.

8. Fold down the top edge.

9. The spike should now be wrapped tightly round and round the shaft. Keep the winding as neat and as tight as possible.

10. To lock the winding, tuck the tip deep into the layers.

11. The Sycamore Seed is complete.

Throwing Tip

To launch, hold the thick spine and throw with force high into the air. It should descend slowly to the ground, spinning rapidly! If it fails to spin well, try launching it by holding a different part of the spine, or by throwing it slightly forwards.

How to design your own planes

For the enthusiast, making and flying the planes in this book will be great fun. However, nothing can quite match the thrill of designing your own plane and seeing it glide effortlessly into the blue yonder. I am convinced that designing paper planes is easier than designing for other origami genres, because a plane only has to fly – it doesn't need to *look like* a dog or a flower or whatever. Thus, the design challenge is simply a mechanical one, not the more problematic aesthetic or representational ones.

Here then, is a beginner's guide.

Be motivated

First, it must be understood that nobody achieves anything without effort. You need to *want* to design a paper plane. With motivation comes patience, a cheerful acceptance of failure and a determination to succeed. If you are only prepared to try it for a few minutes and to give up for ever when your first plane crashes on its maiden flight, then you probably won't design a worthwhile plane.

So ask yourself . . . are you *really* motivated?!

Format

Motivation established, next decide on a paper format. This is usually a simple choice between a square and a rectangle, though you may wish to experiment with strips, triangles and other shapes.

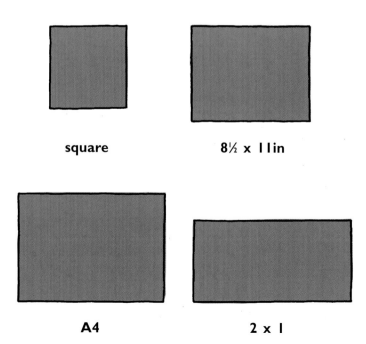

square   **8½ x 11in**

A4   **2 x 1**

Line of symmetry

The choice of where to place that all-important first crease, to establish the line of symmetry, is a surprisingly wide one. Here are some suggestions, though there are others.

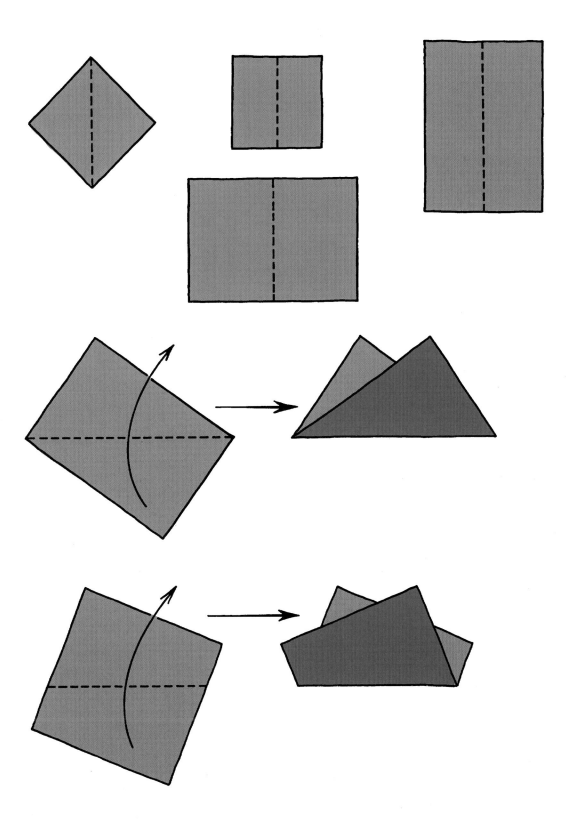

The first few folds

The first few folds are rather like the opening moves – or "gambit" – in a game of chess. There are just a few sensible first moves in chess, after which the number of possible positions for the pieces multiplies with each successive move, until after only a few moves the number of possible positions becomes almost incalculable.

So it is when folding paper. The knack is to establish an end shape for a "folded gambit" which does not necessarily resemble a plane, but which has all the potential of becoming one (or many). Clearly, it is impossible to show all the gambits here (there probably isn't enough paper in the world), so to illustrate the point, here are a series of possible developments – or gambits – from a common opening move.

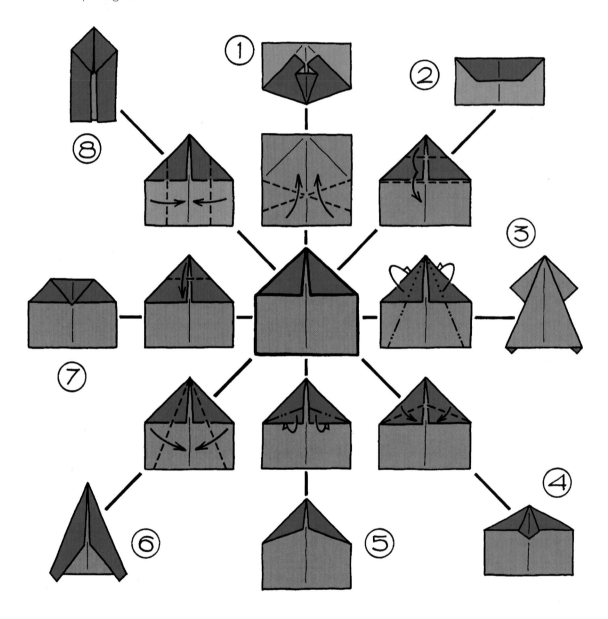

Of course, there are many other developments from the same simple shape, and of the eight shown many could be combined. Similarly, there are many other simple shapes with developmental possibilities, not just those developed from the same line of symmetry crease, but from one of the other creases suggested in the previous section, above. In other words, when all the possible gambits from all the possible line of symmetry creases from all the paper formats are taken into account, the number of shapes possible after just a few folds is immense and will ensure many years of creative exploration.

Bulk the layers at the front

All paper planes of whatever design must be heavier at the front than at the back to give the craft momentum through the air. This is achieved by bulking up the layers towards the nose and thinning them towards the tail. So when designing, remember to pull the layers forward somehow. How this is achieved is a central part of the design.

If too much paper is pulled forward, the excessive weight will make the plane nose-dive; if too little is pulled forward, the craft will stall. Experimentation will tell you just how to distribute the paper to achieve a level flight. Try these variations, then combine them with the different wing shapes and trimming ideas suggested below.

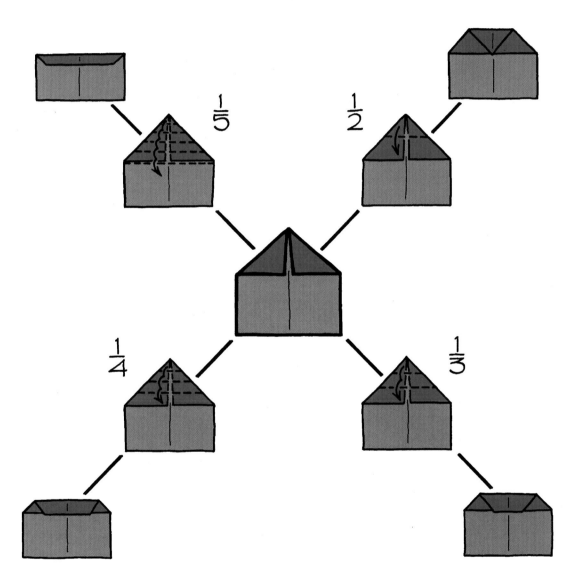

Wing shapes

The shape of the wings makes a surprising difference to the performance of a paper plane. Try these variations with a conventional paper dart to compare performances, then try them with a design of your own creation.

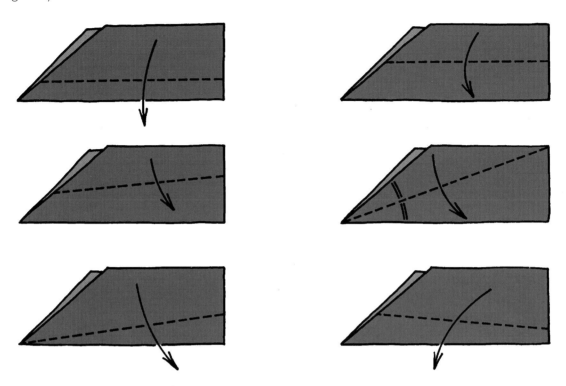

Sometimes, further stability and lift can be gained by adding more creases to the wings. Try these, seen here from the front.

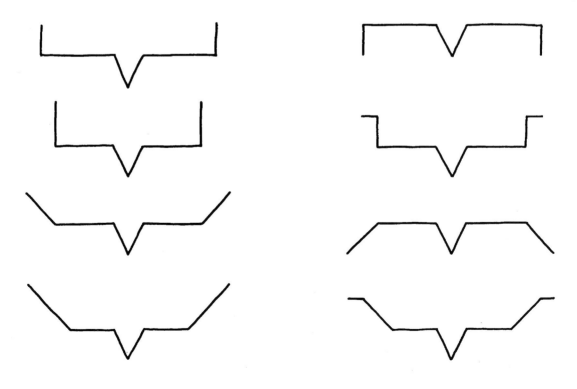

Trimming

Once you have a plane that "feels" like it should fly, it can be trimmed – that is, fiddled with until its profile and speed through the air enables it to fly as well as possible. As before, this can only be achieved with experimentation.

Before trimming a plane, launch it to see how it performs. Read the sections on "Stability" (p. 7) and "My plane won't fly!" (p. 12) for suggestions on how to correct an errant performer. The corrections to consider can be summarised as:

- rolling
- pitching
- yawing
- angle of dihedral
- stalling
- nose-diving
- holding position
- speed of launch
- angle of launch

Remember to fold accurately. Also, a sheet criss-crossed with many experimental creases will never fly well, so fold a fresh version for a true indication of a plane's airworthiness.

Summary

With motivation, patience and a little luck, you *will* succeed in designing an excellent paper plane. If you need a little inspiration, look at some of the designs in this book, perhaps combining ideas from different planes or deliberately trying to do the opposite (however you interpret that) of what is suggested – controlled anarchy is the hallmark of a true creative designer. There is no substitute for experience, so with time your designing will become more fluent and more accurate.

If you doubt whether you can design, just have a go – you have nothing to lose except a few sheets of paper, and the rewards of seeing something that *you* have created flying gracefully from *your* hand are unbeatable.

Acknowledgements

The author would like to thank those Origami Designers who graciously gave permission for their work to be included in this book. Grateful thanks too to Earle Oakes for his magnificent illustrations and for his enthusiasm for the project.

All the designs in this book remain the copyright of the named creator and may not be folded for commercial gain without the written permission of the creator.

Any duplication of previously published designs is entirely coincidental and unintentional.

Contributors:

UK - Robin Glynn, David Morgan, Nick Robinson and John Smith.
USA - Robert Abes, Michael LaFosse, Earle Oakes and Stephen Weiss.
France - Jean-Jerome Casalonga, Alain Georgeot and Eric Joisel.
Brazil - Paolo Immamura.
Japan - Yoshihide Momotani.

Origami Societies

Both of these long-established, friendly organisations cater well for the general origami enthusiast. Membership is inexpensive and worldwide.

British Origami Society
2a The Chestnuts
Countesthorpe
Leicester LE8 5TL
UK

Origami USA
15 West 77th Street
New York
NY 10024–5192
USA